THE EXERCISES OF

Saint Gertrude

THE EXERCISES OF

Saint Gertrude

INTRODUCTION, COMMENTARY AND TRANSLATION

by A Benedictine Nun of Regina Laudis

THE NEWMAN PRESS • WESTMINSTER, MARYLAND

1956

248.22
Ge E

Nihil Obstat: RT. REV. MSGR. JOHN J. BYRNES
Censor Librorum

Imprimatur: HENRY J. O'BRIEN, D.D.
Archbishop of Hartford

Hartford, August 12, 1955

IN GRATITUDE TO OUR REVERED FATHER

RIGHT REVEREND BERNARD KAELIN

ABBOT PRIMATE

OF THE ORDER OF SAINT BENEDICT

THIS BOOK IS DEDICATED

BY

THE PRIORESS AND COMMUNITY

OF REGINA LAUDIS

248.22
GeE

Contents

Introduction

EPIPHANY, the feast of lights, in the year of grace 1256, saw the birth of Saint Gertrude the Great. We catch our first glimpse of her when, some five years later, the gate of the Benedictine Abbey of Helfta, near Eisleben in Saxony, swung open to admit her as a pupil. The name of her family is not recorded, and the reason for this omission has not come down to us either. The little girl crosses the monastic threshold in unexplained loneliness.

Originally founded at Mansfeld, Saxony, in 1229, the community had moved to Helfta only in 1258. The new monastery had been built through the generosity of two wealthy noblemen, Ludwig and Albert von Hackeborn, the brothers of the ruling abbess.[1] The monastic buildings, surrounded by gardens and orchards, stood in a peaceful wooded valley. Several streams crossed the property, widening out to form one of those fish ponds so vital to the medieval monks and nuns. This pond with its limpid waters, overhung by dense foliage and bordered with garden flowers, was to become dear to Gertrude because of the solitude of the place.[2]

Life at Helfta revolved about the abbey church, part of which was screened off as the nuns' choir. The lower part of the walls of this structure, with its twenty-eight ogival lancet windows, most of them long since blocked up, is all that now remains of the former buildings.[3] The outer nave, open to the laity, was often crowded at Mass time;[4] seven candles burned before the altar, as was then customary in a monastic church.[5] In the choir every day the nuns sang the Mass chants and the hours of the Divine Office, given the first place by the Rule of Saint Benedict. And when the bells for Matins broke the silence of night,[6] here they returned to resume their solemn chants of praise, the chantress reading the lessons from a huge book placed on the choir lectern.[7] The choir opened on the cloister, through which the nuns often passed in procession with the crucifix borne before them.[8] Along the cloister they also wended their way after Prime to the chapter house.[9] At the hour of the common repast, they passed through the cloister again, pausing there, after washing their hands in the fountain before they entered the refectory to dine.[10] The abbey had also its dormitories where the nuns had their cells,[11] its domestic offices where they carried on their daily occupations, its barns, and numerous dependencies.[12] In the troublous times, the abbey suffered from various depredations and fell into debt, so that the nuns had additional work to do.[13] The "common work" was too hard for Gertrude, whose health was always delicate, but she was expert at spinning wool.[14] In this brief description of Helfta, the scriptorium and the school must not be forgotten,[15] nor finally the parlors and apartments for guests which were the scene of the traditional hospitality and spiritual works of mercy of the Order of Saint Benedict.[16]

Once inside the abbey, Gertrude found several youthful companions enrolled like herself in the cloister school.[17] Helfta's Lady Abbess, Gertrude von Hackeborn, was possessed of a maturity of character unlooked for in a woman of twenty-seven. Well-educated, adept in administration, gifted for winning hearts, and zealous for that sustained fidelity to the Rule which is known as monastic observance, she maintained a high intellectual standard among her nuns, which gave the monastery an enviable reputation as a center of Christian culture.[18] The curriculum of studies followed in the girls' school included the subjects of the *Trivium*: grammar, rhetoric, and logic; and possibly the *Quadrivium* also: arithmetic, geometry, astronomy, and music. The novices were given a sound training in theology and Scripture by Dominican Friars from Magdeburg or Halle.[19]

As for the little girls, at the time of Gertrude's arrival they were under the direction of the Abbess' twenty-year-old sister, Dame Mechtild von Hackeborn. This first relationship of pupil and mistress between Gertrude and Mechtild was to deepen into a celebrated spiritual friendship between two outstanding saints. Mechtild, the chantress of the abbey, employed her superb voice and musical talent to bring the liturgical chant to the highest peak of beauty. Quick-witted, affable, and sincere, she profited by her charm to draw her fellow nuns after her in the paths of perfection.[20] Gertrude was more predominantly intellectual. Strong of character, she never did anything by halves, and her success in study was so complete that throughout her girlhood and young womanhood, her mental activity gave her the sense of a full life. Having been professed as a nun, she continued to apply herself to the study of the liberal arts and remained enthralled by the charms of classical literature and human wisdom. She found delight in imparting her intellectual riches to others in the community; her pen, fluent alike in German and Latin, was always busy. She spoke as easily as she wrote, and her reputation for learning spread outside the abbey until people of the world began to come knocking at the parlor doors to have speech with her.[21]

At a time and in a manner unknown to us, Dame Mechtild had been raised by God to a mystical life. She was favored with frequent visions in which spiritual realities were presented to her under vividly colorful and pictorial forms. When our Lord or the saints appeared to her, she would converse with them about their earthly lives or the joys of heaven. But all this she took care to conceal, wishing to avoid the prominence which, as the Abbess' sister, would have been hers if her secret had become known.[22]

Meanwhile, probably about 1270, Abbess Gertrude had opened the abbey gate to another Mechtild. The newcomer was an elderly woman who had spent nearly her whole life in Magdeburg as a solitary in prayer and stern penance.[23] Because she had spoken out too boldly about the public scandal given by certain ecclesiastics as well as laymen, a storm had risen against her; and her Dominican directors, who were convinced of her sincerity and heroic virtue, sought a refuge for her at Helfta. Mechtild of Magdeburg was also a mystic. At the age of twelve she had received a mysterious "greeting" from the Holy Spirit which so overpowered her that she forsook her home to give herself entirely to God. She describes herself as unlearned, but nevertheless she possessed poetic gifts of a high order which have been compared to Suso's.[24] The account which she had written in low German of her spiritual experiences had reached the proportions of a book (now known as *The Flowing Light of the Godhead*); she brought it with her and completed it at Helfta, where she spent the remaining twelve years of her life. Courageous in embracing the monastic life in her old age, she was yet more deeply sanctified by it; and she in turn imparted to the two saints of Helfta something of the lyrical freshness of her poetic inspiration, which added a new element to the monastic tradition they had breathed since childhood. Both Gertrude and Dame Mechtild venerated her and voiced their faith in her holiness and in the God-given character of her writings.[25]

Nothing suggests, however, that the example of Mechtild of Magdeburg had set Gertrude pining for mystical experiences of her own. She was absorbed in the school; to all appearances she had never been more than ordinarily pious. Her first contact with the supernatural world on January 27, 1281, came as a surprise. In the dormitory after Compline, without warning, our Lord appeared to her and told her that He Himself would help her to lead a more fervent life.[26] With her characteristic energy, Gertrude promptly renounced all secular studies. More gradually, she came to renounce herself as well.

For a short time, however, she asked herself if all this could be true; and in her doubt, she confided in Dame Mechtild, who reassured her, as she was well qualified to do.[27] It was not until after the death of Abbess Gertrude, however, that Dame Mechtild in turn confided to Gertrude some of the countless visions which she had been keeping secret over so many years.

In 1289, at Christ's command, Gertrude had written in Latin a short autobiographical account of her new-found spiritual life, to which her fellow nuns later added all the information they could obtain from or about her. This composite book is known as the *Herald of Divine Love,* or the *Revelations of Saint Gertrude.* With the collaboration of another nun, Gertrude also composed, some time after 1292, a book relating Dame Mechtild's visions, entitled the *Book of Special Grace.*[28] Dame Mechtild died in 1298, and Gertrude in 1301 or 1302. Through the Dominicans, the *Book of Special Grace* had a rapid diffusion. It was even translated into English, not later than the early fifteenth century, being known as the *Book of Saint Maud* or the *Book of Ghostly Grace.*[29] Dame Mechtild soon acquired an aura of sanctity, completely eclipsing Gertrude, who was not to come into her own until after the invention of printing. In 1505 Gertrude's *Herald* was printed at Leipzig in a German translation. From the appearance of the first Latin edition in 1536, her fame was assured. Neither Saint Gertrude nor Saint Mechtild has ever been formally canonized. An office in honor of Saint Gertrude was first authorized by Rome in 1606; her name was inserted in the Roman Martyrology in 1678, but Saint Mechtild's is not found there. The feast of Saint Gertrude was extended to the universal Church by Clement XII in 1738.

The Exercises of Saint Gertrude

The only other extant work of Gertrude's pen is her masterpiece, the *Exercises*. Editions of it have been rare, and it remains less well known than the *Herald*. This is a pity. Gertrude herself plainly attached importance to the little book. Its carefully balanced structure and its style, characterized by elaborate word patterns, bear witness to the hours she devoted to its composition. She wove into it innumerable phrases from the Scriptures, the loving study of which had replaced her onetime enthusiasm for secular learning. And into it, in the full maturity of her powers, she poured her deepest reflections and aspirations. Above all, throughout these pages, she is the mystic to whom the supernatural world is familiar through personal and frequent experience.

Extraordinary graces were bestowed on Gertrude from the night when Christ first appeared to her. Her visions seem to have been far less numerous and far less pictorial than those of Saint Mechtild; but she was granted the stigmata in 1284,[30] and some time later received in her heart the wound of love,[31] which exceedingly lofty favors, as Dom Castel points out, were not accorded to Saint Mechtild.[32] Gertrude enjoyed the continual awareness of the Divine presence and reached a high degree of the transforming union.

Gertrude's spirituality is above all Trinitarian and Christocentric. No doubt the sound doctrinal training of the Dominicans had been willed by God as the orientation from which, when His hour struck, He would make her advance so rapidly. The loving Fatherhood of God, the sonship of adoption, the indwelling and sanctifying action of the Holy Spirit are all living realities to Gertrude. Reverently she contemplates the Divine attributes, in the light of which she sees more and more profoundly into the depths of God's vast plan for the incarnation of the Word and the redemption of the human race.

To the Rule's repeated injunction, "Prefer nothing to the

love of Christ," [33] Gertrude responds with a devotion to the Saviour so pure, so ardent, and so generous, that she ranks among the greatest lovers of Christ in the annals of sainthood. The primacy of His love is bound up with the revelation of His Sacred Heart, which was made to her, as well as to Saint Mechtild, four hundred years before Saint Margaret Mary's day. Holy Communion was the object of Gertrude's unspeakable desire and reverence. The mystical marriage with Christ to which she was raised, is the theme of her amazed thanksgivings. Her love for the Divine Bridegroom centers particularly on His sufferings; the passion was one of her chief subjects of meditation.[34]

By nature Gertrude was inclined to be domineering;[35] but grace led her in the paths of humility and docility to Christ. In her account of her first vision—one of the most poignant pages of all autobiography—she tells us that He said to her: "Thou hast licked the earth among My enemies, and thou hast sucked honey among thorns; but now at last return to Me, and I will inebriate thee with the torrent of My Divine delights." While He was saying this, she saw between herself and Him an endless hedge, the top of which was so bristling with thorns that she could discover no way of returning to Him. While she hesitated, our Lord suddenly reached out to her and with no difficulty lifted her over the hedge.[36] Gertrude understood that the thorny hedge represented the interest in secular studies with which her heart had, until then, been filled, to the detriment of her life as a nun. She felt a keen sorrow for what she believed to be her sins, and this humble contrition she never lost. Like Saint Mechtild, she does not weary of proclaiming that, after we have done our best to be faithful to God's demands, we must still depend on Christ to atone for our shortcomings and perfect the efforts of our virtues. And she insists again and again on the mystical death; we must leave not only our faults and attachments, but even our very selves, and pass over from ourselves into God, in the death to self and the death in God so dear to the greatest mystics.

Not the least striking note of Gertrude's spirituality is her lofty purity of soul. There is a virginal quality in all her attitudes of mind. She is undividedly God's. Hence no flight is too high for her, and nothing holds her back; she soars towards heaven without restraint. The Divine eternity draws her irresistibly. She has entered into the love for "eternal life" to which Saint Benedict so often returns in his Rule.[37] One favor she received was an intellectual vision of God, to which authorities on mysticism attach great importance, wherein she mysteriously beheld the invisible face of the Lord.[38] This faint foretaste of the Beatific Vision no doubt intensified the longing with which she speaks so often of seeing the face of God, the countenance of God, as her ultimate and supreme goal.

Finally in Gertrude's spirituality one may point to its simplicity. Having literally grown up in the cloister, Gertrude was formed by the daily chant of the psalms, the tranquil round of monastic observance, and the ever-recurring liturgical feasts through which the Church guides her children again and again through the mysteries of Christ's life. Gertrude does not seek her spirituality outside this providential framework. She rather intensifies the life that is planned for her by Saint Benedict in the Rule, finding the most sublime union with God by fulfilling the monastic duty of singing His praise day and night and glorifying Him in all things.

One curious mistake about Saint Gertrude must be pointed out again. Through the slip of a heedless historian in 1595,[39] she was confused with Gertrude von Hackeborn and therefore supposed to have been the Abbess of Helfta. This error was exposed some three hundred years later by Dom Paquelin of Solesmes;[40] but having been widespread for so long, it is still to be met with in references to Gertrude and particularly in art, where she is nearly always represented with the crozier that was never hers.

Was Gertrude a "black" Benedictine or a Cistercian? This question has raised not a little discussion. From the still extant charters of Helfta, we know that the original foundation in 1229 was made by Cistercian nuns.[41] The new monastery did not, however, belong to the Cistercian Order and was not under the jurisdiction of the white monks, for just a year earlier the General Chapter had decreed that no more communities of nuns should be either founded or directed by the Order. It follows that Helfta must have been one of the many autonomous abbeys of Benedictine nuns that flourished in Germany in the thirteenth century. Gertrude's latest editor, Dom Pierre Doyère, states that in her day the discipline and spirituality of Helfta were undoubtedly of Cistercian inspiration, while at the same time, thanks to its independence, the monastery observed certain customs of its own.[42]

Saint Gertrude's *Exercises* consist of prayers and reflections, the haunting beauty of which can best be appreciated by a perusal, in order, of the entire book. These prayers are divided into seven different "exercises" or chapters, which turn on the following themes: baptism, investiture (reception of the monastic habit), spiritual espousals, monastic profession, praise of God, and preparation for death. Gertrude proposes that the first four Exercises should be repeated annually, as devotional renewals of the red letter days which they commemorate; she seems to have intended the last three Exercises for more frequent use. For the assistance of our readers, each of these chapters will be introduced by a few pages of commentary, giving an outline of the contents and some explanation of the background and points of special interest or difficulty.

The learned and widely travelled Alban Butler, who was one of the warmest admirers of the *Exercises,* wrote more than two hundred years ago: "We have a living portraiture of [Gertrude's] pure and holy soul in her short book." [43] A painstaking comparison of the *Exercises* with the three other books from Helfta—the *Herald of Divine Love,* the *Book of Special Grace,* and the *Flowing Light of the Godhead*—gives a fuller meaning to that felicitous remark. It seems to be clear that the devotional "renewals" found in the *Exercises* reveal Saint Gertrude's and Saint Mechtild's own spiritual practices. No doubt Saint Gertrude wished to benefit her fellow nuns by these writings, but at the same time she gives us an insight into the customs she herself observed. The passages from the books of Helfta that are interrelated with the *Exercises* will be brought together in the commentary on the chapters which they illustrate.

An additional example of the cutom of devotional renewals as practised by our two saints, is afforded in connection with a book composed by Saint Gertrude which has not come down to us. This was her *Remembrance of Death,* a sort of retreat of five days, intended to be made "at least once a year" as a preparation for death.[44] We read in chapter 4 of the last book of the *Herald of Divine Love* that as Saint Mechtild lay in bed during her last illness, about a month before her death (which occurred on November 19, 1298), "she was anxious, according to her habitual custom of devotion and good will, to solemnize the *Remembrance of Death* which Gertrude had composed. And . . . on Sunday, through the reception of the most holy Body and Blood of Christ, she entrusted to His Divine mercy the final hour when she should breathe forth her spirit." [45] We are certain, therefore, that Saint Mechtild habitually used this work of Gertrude's for her own spiritual needs.

In the narrative of Saint Gertrude's last year on earth, in chapter 27 of the same book of the *Herald,* we learn that after she received, on Easter Wednesday, a Divine injunction to use the short time of life that remained to her in making ready for death, she, in turn, resolved "as she had taught her instructions on death to others, to use them again herself." She was so much concerned to profit by her retreat, that she began with three days of prayer to obtain the grace to carry it out devoutly. After this, she spent the following five days, according to the plan of her book, meditating on the subjects of last illness, confession, extreme unction, viaticum, and death, carefully reciting the prayers which she had appointed for each day. Apparently the retreat was meant to begin on a Wednesday, since it was on a Sunday that Gertrude, like Mechtild, concluded her retreat by recalling "the day when she should finally breathe forth her spirit." [46]

It is characteristic of Saint Gertrude, as every reader of the *Exercises* will see for himself, that on the following Sunday "she solemnized that most joyful festival on which, after leaving this land of exile, she should take her place for the first time in the presence of the Most Blessed Trinity," [47] beholding at last the eternal glory of her Lord Jesus Christ whom she had seen, whom she had loved, in whom she had believed, whom she had loved exceedingly.

REGINA LAUDIS, O.S.B.
Bethlehem, Connecticut
Feast of the Most Holy Trinity
June 5, 1955

Translator's Note

THE AIM of this new translation is to present Saint Gertrude's
all too neglected spiritual classic in a form accessible to the
modern reader. The Latin edition used by the translator is that
of the Abbey of Saint Mary's of Praglia.[1] The original text has
been reverently treated, and limited attempts have even been
made to find an equivalent for the word patterns of Gertrude's
lyrical prose. In a few instances where the sense can be clarified
by a slight expansion, a word or two have been inserted, in
most cases following the treatment of these passages in the
French translation by Dom Guéranger. In the fourth Exercise
there are two obvious omissions in the Latin text; the first, that
of Psalm 33, has been supplied by the translator; the second,
that of the antiphon after Psalm 90, is given as it appears in
the latest French translation, and "rubrics" are inserted before
each psalm following the same authority.[2]

Saint Gertrude's fondness for scriptural expressions and
loosely paraphrased texts creates a special problem in the
method of translation. If every recognizable allusion were ren-
dered in the phraseology of the Douay version, the stilted effect
would be far from pleasing. The translator has therefore been
advised by competent authority to render fragmentary quotations and loose paraphrases somewhat freely, while giving the
references for every scriptural allusion. All literal quotations of

more than one verse in length are taken from the Douay version. In the canticle of Simeon, however, the word "release" has been substituted for "dismiss," on the authority of the Confraternity edition of the psalms.[3] This change is made in order to bring out the meaning of Gertrude's prayer inspired by this canticle, where the English word "dismiss" fails to convey the sense.

To simplify the commentary, a list of the liturgical texts which are quoted by Saint Gertrude has been placed at the back of the book.

Sincere thanks for the procuring or loan of reference books and items of information are extended to: the Abbot of Solesmes; the Benedictine Fathers of Saint John's Abbey, Collegeville; Dom Pierre Doyère, O.S.B.; Reverend M. Laurence Bourget, O.C.S.O.; Reverend Irenaeus Herscher, O.F.M.; Reverend Columban Duffy, O.F.M.; the Lady Abbess of Jouarre; Sister Florence Feeney, O.S.B.; Mother Marion Mooney, R.C.; Mrs. Hastings H. Hart; Miss Ruth M. Gordon; Mr. R. A. Wilson of the British Museum; Mr. B. A. Dunne of London; Mr. Lloyd B. Holsapple; Mr. Paul Myers; and several other friends. Special acknowledgment is made to Miss Ruth Michael, of Wellesley College, who most kindly read the entire typescript of the translation and made many valuable suggestions.

To complete the history of the *Exercises,* the following list of editions has been compiled from the sources of information available: [4]

The Latin manuscript possessed by John Lanspergius, the Carthusian of Cologne, apparently no longer exists, and no other manuscript has been discovered. The first printed edition of the work is that of Lanspergius, published at Cologne in 1536. The other Latin editions are as follows: Madrid, 1599 (edited by Dom John Castagniza, O.S.B.); Salzburg, 1662 (edited by Dom Lawrence Clement, O.S.B.); Paris, 1666 (edited by Dom Joseph Mège, the Maurist); Angers, 1862 (edited by Dom Guéranger); Paris, 1875 (edited by Dom Paquelin, O.S.B., of Solesmes); Padua, 1924 (edited by the monks of the Abbey of Saint Mary's of Praglia). The Italian editions are: Venice, 1560 (translated by Vincenzo Buondi); Padua, 1924 (translated by the monks of the Abbey of Saint Mary's of Praglia). The French editions are: Paris, 1580 (J. Jarry); Paris, 1621 (translated by René Gualtier); Paris, 1672 (anonymous translator); Paris, 1862 (translated by Dom Guéranger; this work has passed through nine editions); Paris, 1919 (translated by Abbot Emmanuel); Paris, 1942 (translated by Dom Albert Schmitt, O.S.B., of Solesmes). The first Spanish edition is that of Salamanca, 1605 (translated by Dom Leander de Granade y Mendoca, O.S.B.). A German translation by Dom Maurus Wolter appeared almost simultaneously with that of Dom Guéranger in 1863 and went through nine editions; a new version by Dom Willibrord Verkade, O.S.B., was published in Freiburg in 1936. The English translation by the Reverend Thomas Alder Pope, Priest of the Birmingham Oratory, was contemporary with that of Dom Maurus Wolter; the latest of its many editions was published in London in 1927.

1st Exercise

TO REGAIN BAPTISMAL INNOCENCE

Commentary

IT IS tempting to draw a certain comparison between the *Exercises* of Saint Gertrude and the Rule of Saint Benedict, for both books begin with the Divine adoption and guide us onward and upward from this beginning to the summits of perfection. Here once more Gertrude shows herself to be a representative of the monastic tradition. But she is not merely reciting a lesson that she has been taught; rather, she speaks from the conviction of her faith, enlivened and enlightened by her gift of contemplation. In this relatively short book, she calls upon God no less than thirteen times, in the words of the psalmist, as "God of my life!" To her, Christ, who is God, is the source of our true life; by living that life on earth, to the best of our ability and in constant dependence on Christ, we shall attain in heaven to that perfect union with the Triune God which is the plenitude of eternal life. This is Gertrude's message, which she will present from many angles as she unfolds to us the wonder of Christ's mysteries; the heights of our calling to the perfection of charity, contrasted with the depths of our unworthiness; and the glory of heaven which is the dwelling-place of God.

Our Divine adoption through Christ, as sons of the Father, and our participation in the life of God, are inaugurated by the sacrament of baptism. This is why Gertrude begins her *Exercises* by inviting us to a spiritual renewal of our own baptism.

To this end, she reminds us of the various ceremonies which accompany the administration of the sacrament. Guiding us by quaint rubrics, a device which she follows throughout the book, she makes us pass meditatively from one ceremony to another. Having recalled the Creed, the exorcism, the marking with the sign of the cross, the imposition of the priest's hand (after which she inserts a prayer to the guardian angel), and the placing of salt on the tongue, she turns to our Lady and asks her to become her "Godmother." This exquisite prayer gives a first insight into the unself-consciousness, depth, and beauty of her devotion to Mary. She then goes on to the conferring of the baptismal name, the immersion in the font, the anointing with chrism, and the presentation of the lighted candle and the white garment.

To the present-day reader, the most puzzling passage in the first Exercise will no doubt be the next to the last paragraph, where Gertrude plays on the word "Amen." Abbot Emmanuel, in his notes on the *Exercises,* is at pains to provide an explanation. The word "Amen," he tells us, means, "It is true." Gertrude here takes it in the sense of "Truth"—the eternal Truth which is God Himself.[1] If the prayer is reread with this substitution, its meaning becomes clear.

1st Exercise

TO REGAIN BAPTISMAL INNOCENCE

If thou dost desire to present before God at the close of thy life the robe of thy baptismal innocence unspotted and the seal of the Christian faith whole and unimpaired, be thou careful at some appointed season, chiefly at Eastertide and Pentecost, to solemnize the memory of thy baptism. Stir up thy desire, therefore, to be reborn in God by the holiness of a new life and to be restored unto a new childhood, using these words:

May God be merciful unto me and bless me; may He enlighten me with the light of His countenance and be merciful unto me.[1] Let my heart bless Him in all sincerity and truth. Let the earth of my heart tremble before the face of the Lord;[2] by the Spirit of His mouth, let my spirit be created anew and restored,[3] that His good Spirit may lead me into the land of righteousness.[4]

Then read the Creed, "I believe in God," praying unto the Lord that He may make thee utterly renounce Satan and may keep thee in true, living, and perfect faith even unto the end of thy life.

[1] Cf. Ps. 66:2. [2] Cf. Ps. 113:7. [3] Cf. Ps. 103:30.
[4] Cf. Ps. 142:10.

[5]

PRAYER

O Lord God, holy and true, my Creator and my Redeemer, who hast signed me with the holy light of Thy countenance,[5] redeemed me at the dear price of the blood of Thy Only Begotten, and regenerated me unto the hope of life[6] through baptism in the power of Thy Spirit, make me renounce Satan and all his pomps and all his works in very truth, with a sincere and perfect heart. Make me faithfully believe, with true and burning faith crowned with living works, in Thee, my God and my Creator, through Jesus Christ Thy Son, who is the way, the truth, and the life,[7] in the might of the Holy Spirit. And cause me to cleave unto Thee and to go steadfastly with Thee unto the end. Amen.

To renew the seal of thy faith, say these words:

O holy Trinity, Father, and Son, and Holy Spirit, may Thy divine omnipotence rule and confirm my faith, Thy divine wisdom instruct and enlighten it, and Thy divine goodness help and perfect it, that at the hour of my death I may render up this my faith undefiled and unaltered before Thy face, together with all the virtues which it will have gained for me.

Recalling the exorcism, pray unto the Lord that in the power of His name He will make thee prudently overcome and perceive all the cunning tricks of Satan, that the enemy may never pride himself on having conquered thee, but may himself withdraw vanquished in every temptation and discomfited at the first encounter:

PRAYER

O Lord Jesus Christ, Thou High Priest, who by Thy precious death didst give me life, deign with Thy breath in the power of Thy Spirit to rid me of all the wiles of the enemy by the efficacy of Thy presence. Rend asunder within me all the snares of

[5] Cf. Ps. 4:7.   [6] Cf. 1 Pet. 1:3.   [7] Cf. John 14:6.

Satan, and by Thy pitying glance banish from me all blindness of heart. O Christ, may Thy perfect charity make me triumph manfully over every temptation. May Thy holy humility teach me to shun with prudence all the snares of the enemy. May Thy radiant truth lead me onward and make me walk before Thee with a sincere and perfect heart. And may the blessing of Thy most forgiving mercy precede, follow, and keep me unto the end of my life. Amen.

Here thou shalt make the sign of the holy cross upon thy brow and upon thy breast, saying these words:

In the name of the Father, and of the Son, and of the Holy Ghost. O dearest Jesus, my crucified Love, let me receive from Thee the sign of Thy holy cross, both upon my brow and upon my heart, that I may live eternally under Thy protection. Give me living faith in Thy heavenly precepts, that I may run in the way of Thy commandments with my heart open wide.[8] Through Thy help may I so conduct myself that I may deserve to become the temple of God and the dwelling place of the Holy Spirit. Amen.

Now earnestly request that Jesus Christ the High Priest may Himself lay His hand upon thee, that thou mayest dwell for ever in the shelter of the Most High and abide under the protection of the God of heaven:

O most loving Jesus, protect me beneath the shadow of Thy hand;[9] let Thy right hand sustain me.[10] Open unto me the door of Thy love, that having been dedicated with the seal of Thy wisdom, I may in truth be free from all earthly desire, serve Thee with joy in Thy holy Church according to the sweet odor of Thy precepts, and daily advance from strength unto strength.[11] Amen.

[8] Cf. Ps. 118:32.   [9] Cf. Isai. 49:2.
[10] Cf. Ps. 17:36.   [11] Ps. 83:8.

Now beseech the Lord to give thee an angel who will guide thee upon thy way:

O Jesus, Prince of Peace [12] and Angel of the Great Counsel, be Thou Thyself my guide on my right hand and the guardian of my pilgrimage, that I may not be driven backwards or wander away from Thee; and deign to send Thy holy angel from heaven, who under Thy loving command will direct me according to Thy good pleasure and by Thy pathway bring me back, perfect, unto Thee. Amen.

Now say this prayer to receive and greet thy angel:

Hail, holy angel of God, guardian of my soul and body! Through the most sweet Heart of Jesus Christ the Son of God, for love of Him who created both thee and me, for love of Him who entrusted me unto thee at my baptism, take me under thy most faithful and fatherly care. Thanks to thy assistance, may I pass through the seething torrent of this life without defilement, until with thee I attain with joy unto the vision of that glorious countenance (which thou dost already behold) and that most enrapturing beauty of the sovereign Godhead, which surpasseth the sweetness of all felicity.

Now pray that thy mouth may be filled with the salt of wisdom, that thou mayest perceive the taste of faith in the Holy Spirit:

Let me receive from Thee, O sweetest Jesus, through Thy mercy, the salt of wisdom and the spirit of understanding unto eternal life. Amen.

Grant me experience of the sweetness of Thy Spirit; grant me hunger for Thy will; and grant me knowledge of Thy good pleasure, that my service may ever be acceptable unto Thee. Amen.

[12] Isai. 9:6.

*Now make the sign of the holy cross upon thy ears and
nostrils and pray unto the Lord, that He Himself may open
the ears of thy heart unto His law, and fill thy entire being
with the fragrance of knowledge of Himself:*

O Jesus, Thou Shepherd beloved of my heart, come, grant
that I, Thy unworthy little ewe lamb, may ever recognize and
follow Thy dulcet voice.[13] Grant that drawn by the strong perfume of living faith, I may run to the pastures of eternal life,
and there, through all eternity, be still and see, O my Lord,
how truly Thou art sweet.

*Take in thy right hand the standard of the life-giving cross,
wherewith to conquer the enemy, and say:*

O most loving Jesus, place in my right hand the banner of
Thy holy cross. Let my hand ever be armed with this banner
as I advance against all the ambuscades of the enemy, and let
me be surrounded by the rampart of Thy assistance. Amen.

May the omnipotence of God the Father bless me. May the
wisdom of the Son bless me. May the most benign charity of
the Holy Ghost bless me and keep me unto everlasting life.
Amen.

*Then shalt thou pray the Virgin Mother to obtain for thee
a perfect renewal of thy life. May she, that rose worthy of
all reverence, become by this favor both thy Mother and
thy Godmother. Be thou a true daughter unto her in all
that thou dost. And may she, that jewel of purity, keep thy
soul wrapped, under her gentle gaze, in the mantle of her
modesty, and immaculate in the sight of that King, our
Lord, who is her Son. May she also bring it to pass that
thou be numbered with Israel; then shall thy part be with
them who walk in innocence of heart,[14] keeping the Lord
ever before their eyes in all their ways:*

[13] Cf. John 10:27.   [14] Cf. Ps. 100:2.

[9]

Hail, Mary, thou Queen of clemency and olive tree of mercy, through whom came unto us the healing of life! Hail, Queen of clemency! Hail, Virgin Mother of the Divine Branch, through whom came unto us He who is heavenly light, the Branch of the fragrance of Israel! Through thy Son thou didst become the true Mother of all men, for thy only Son did not disdain to become their Brother; now for love of Him, take me, unworthy as I am, under thy motherly care. Succor my faith, preserve it, and build it up, and thus become the Godmother of my renewal and of my faith at this moment, so that in eternity thou mayest be my one and most dearly beloved Mother; and having watched over me with merciful constancy in this life, admit me unto the plenitude of thy motherhood at the hour of my death. Amen.

As thou callest to mind the conferring of thy baptismal name:

O sweetest Jesus, set down my name beneath Thy glorious name in the book of life. Say unto my soul: "Thou art Mine; I, Thy salvation, have acknowledged thee! Now thou shalt no more be called *Forsaken,* but thou shalt be called *My pleasure in her,*[15] that My inheritance may be with thee for ever in the land of the living."[16]

Now recall how thou wast immersed in the font, in the name of the Father, and of the Son, and of the Holy Ghost:

O Jesus, fountain of life, come, give me to drink a cup of the living water[17] which floweth from Thee, that once I have tasted Thee, I may nevermore thirst save for Thee. Immerse my whole being in the depths of Thy mercy. Baptize me in the spotlessness of Thy precious death. Renew me in Thy blood, wherewith Thou hast redeemed me. In the water from Thy most holy side, wash away every stain wherewith I have ever

[15] Isai. 62:4.   [16] Cf. Ps. 141:6.   [17] Cf. John 4:10.

sullied my baptismal innocence. Fill me with Thy Spirit and take possession of my whole being in purity both of body and of soul. Amen.

In remembrance of the chrism, pray unto the Lord that the anointing of His Spirit may teach thee concerning all things: [18]

O Father most holy, who through Thy Son, our Lord Jesus Christ, hast caused me to be born again of water and of the Holy Spirit; grant me today the full remission of all my sins, and deign to anoint me with the chrism of Thy Spirit unto eternal life. Amen. May Thy peace be with me for evermore. Amen.

Here make the sign of the holy cross upon thy breast and upon thy shoulders, saying:

Let me always bear upon my shoulders, for love of Thy love, the sweet yoke and light burden [19] of Thy commandments and constantly taste the mystery of holy faith like a bundle of myrrh [20] upon my breast, that Thou who wast crucified for me mayest abide ever impressed upon my heart. Amen.

In remembrance of the white garment which was given thee, say:

O Jesus, Sun of Justice, come, let me clothe myself in Thee,[21] that I may live as Thou wouldst have me live. Let me so follow Thee that I may keep the garment of my baptismal innocence white, holy, and unspotted, and bring it unimpaired before Thy judgment seat, to keep it unto eternal life. Amen.

Recalling how thou didst receive the lighted candle, pray for inward illumination:

O Jesus, Thou light that shalt never fail, come, enkindle in me the burning lamp of Thy unfailing charity and teach me to

[18] Cf. 1 John 2:27. [19] Cf. Matt. 11:30.
[20] Cant. 1:12. [21] Cf. Rom. 13:14.

keep my baptism without blame; that when I am summoned unto Thy marriage feast,[22] being found ready, I may deserve to enter upon the delights of eternal life, beholding Thee, the true light, and the glorious face of Thy Godhead. Amen.

In remembrance of thy holy Communion, wherein thou didst receive the life-giving Body and Blood of the spotless Lamb, Jesus Christ, say:

O Jesus Christ, my Lord, may Thy adorable Body and Thy precious Blood keep my body and my soul unto eternal life. Amen. May Thy peace be with me. O Jesus, true Peace, in Thee may I have for evermore peace upon peace, until through Thee I reach that peace which surpasseth all understanding,[23] where, rejoicing in Thee, I shall behold Thee for all eternity. Amen.

In this holy Communion, desire that thy whole life may be hidden with Christ in God,[24] and that in the hour of thy death thou mayest be found entirely perfect:

O Jesus, my dearest Beloved, sweetest guest of my soul, may Thy gracious presence within me be unto me today the remission of all my sins; may it atone for all my shortcomings and regain all the losses of my poor life. May it be my eternal salvation, the restoration of my soul and body, the enkindling of my love, the renewal of my virtues, and the everlasting ending of my life in Thee.

May it be unto me liberty of spirit, soundness of life, and purity of manners. May it be unto me a shield of patience, a badge of humility, a staff of trust, a solace in sadness, and a help unto perseverance. May it be unto me the armor of faith, the strength of hope, the perfection of charity, the fulfilment of Thy commandments, renewal of spirit, sanctification in truth,[25] and the perfection of my whole monastic life.

22 Cf. Matt. 22:3; Apoc. 19:7.   23 Phil. 4:7.
24 Cf. Col. 3:3.   25 Cf. John 17:17.

May it be unto me the source of virtues, the end of vices, the increase of all gifts, and the deathless covenant of Thy love, that while I dwell only corporeally in this land of exile, my thoughts may constantly turn in longing meditation thither where Thou art, Thou my surpassing inheritance. Then at the end of my life, when once I have cast off the most bitter outward rind of this body, I shall attain unto that sweetest fruit, where in the new light of Thy glorious Manhood I may see the most dazzling splendor of Thy most sublime Godhead, where the all-fair rose of Thy glorious face shall refresh me with its royal beauty, where after I have laid aside the troubles of this life I shall feast in joy for ever and exult in the riches of Thy charity as a bride rejoiceth in the delights of her king. Amen.

In remembrance of the sacrament of confirmation, say:

O Jesus, most victorious King and great High Priest, confirm me by Thy almighty power and gird me with the sword of the Spirit, O Thou most mighty,[26] that I may ever be victorious over the thousand wiles of Satan, and all my victory may be in Thee.

Thou shalt conclude by this request:

O Lord my God, who wast my Creator that Thou mightest also be my Restorer, renew today Thy Holy Spirit within me and enroll me among Thy people of adoption as a newborn infant; that with the children of the promise, I may rejoice at having received by grace what I do not possess by nature.

Make me great in faith; joyful in hope; patient in tribulation; full of delight in Thy praise; fervent in the Spirit; faithful to serve Thee, my Lord, my God, and my true King; and vigilant to persevere with Thee unto the end of my life. Then what I now believe in hope, my eyes shall joyfully behold in reality; then I shall see Thee as Thou art, I shall behold Thee face to

26 Cf. Eph. 6:17; Ps. 44:4.

face. Then, dearest Jesus, Thou wilt make me like unto Thyself; then I shall find eternal rest in the fruition of Thy glorious countenance. Amen. Amen. Amen.

May this God most faithful, this Amen most true, He who never faileth, make me ardently thirst for the dear Amen whereby He awakeneth love; pleasantly taste the delightful Amen whereby He giveth refreshment; and be happily perfected by that redeeming Amen whereby He imparteth beatitude; [27] that I may effectually deserve to experience for evermore the eternal and most sweet Amen,[28] whereby I believe that after this exile I shall behold that true Amen [29] Himself, Jesus, the Son of God, who alone can give unto His beloved perfect contentment, and who, together with the Father and the Holy Spirit, bestoweth all blessings and despiseth not that which He created. Amen. Amen. Amen.

By the following prayer, commit unto the Lord thy faith and thy baptismal innocence:

O my dearest Jesus, take the purity of my baptismal innocence and the written bond of my faith into the safekeeping of Thy most benign Heart, that thanks to Thy faithful guardianship, I may present them unto Thee unimpaired at the hour of my death. I pray Thee to imprint the seal of Thy Heart upon my heart, that I may live as Thou wouldst have me live, and after this exile be in no way prevented from coming joyfully unto Thee. Amen.

[27] See Apoc. 7:12.   [28] *Ibid.* 19:4.   [29] *Ibid.* 3:14.

2nd Exercise

SPIRITUAL CONVERSION

Commentary

INVESTITURE is, for the nun, the first solemn ceremony of her monastic life, in which she lays aside for ever the apparel of the world and puts on the austere religious habit. The title "Spiritual Conversion" given to the second Exercise by Saint Gertrude refers to Saint Benedict's use of the word "conversion" in his Rule, where he applies it to entrance into the monastery.[1] In the early days of the monastic Orders, a nun's investiture might take place at practically the same time as her entrance; thus an ancient feast in honor of the investiture of Saint Radegunde (d. 578) was known as "Saint Radegunde's Conversion."

Saint Gertrude proposes this Exercise for the anniversary of investiture. If it was her custom to solemnize the memory of her own investiture on the recurrence of the day, it would seem that she took the habit on an Easter Monday. It was on this day that as she prayed our Lord to atone, by the merits of the Holy Eucharist, for her past negligence in the observances of the Order, she beheld a vision in which:

> the Son of God took her and presented her to God the Father. She was clothed in the monastic habit, which seemed to be made of as many pieces as she had lived years in the monastic state. The lower piece of the habit represented the first year, the second piece the second

year, and so on to the year then current. And the habit seemed to be so wide and so long that not the suggestion of a fold could be found anywhere in it, but in each separate year the days and hours might be seen written down, with each and every thought, word, and deed, good or bad, which had been hers in that year from day to day, from hour to hour, from thought to thought, from word to word, from deed to deed. Then when our Lord offered for her to the Father His most innocent and most perfect earthly life, the habit seemed to be covered with plates of shining gold.[2]

Most writers of the last few decades are of the opinion that Gertrude and her fellow nuns received the white Cistercian habit.[3] Saint Mechtild comments on the wide sleeves of the tunic, saying that they symbolize generosity of heart.[4] Mechtild for her own part was contented with a habit covered with patches and darns; she accepted only under protest a veil of fine material (assigned her perhaps in order to relieve her violent headaches).[5] Gertrude was noted for her readiness to accept the clothing offered her without stopping to consider whether it was desirable or not.[6]

This shortest of all the Exercises is easy to follow. The phrase "school of the Holy Spirit" is another allusion to the Rule, where Saint Benedict calls the monastery "a school of the Lord's service."[7] In the prayer to our Lady beginning, "O Mary, Mother of God," the phrase about the fleece of the true Lamb is echoed in the *Herald* in one of Saint Gertrude's visions.[8] The liturgical responsory "The kingdom of the world" is of special interest because it recurs in the third and fourth Exercises.

2nd Exercise

SPIRITUAL CONVERSION

FOR THE ANNIVERSARY OF INVESTITURE WITH THE HOLY HABIT

Whenever thou renewest thy good purpose, desiring to solemnize the memory of thy first conversion whereby thou didst renounce the world and to convert thy heart with its whole strength unto God, thou shalt use this exercise. Let thy prayer be that God may build up for Himself within thee a monastery of love and of all the virtues; and first thou shalt say:

O Jesus, Thou dearest Beloved of my heart, it is most true that no spiritual fruit can be borne without being watered by the dew of Thy Spirit and ripened by the heat of Thy love. Have pity on me then, take me into the arms of Thy love, and warm my whole being by Thy Spirit! Behold, I give over my body and my soul into Thy keeping to be Thy possession.

O my Beloved, pour forth Thy blessing upon me. Open unto me the treasure house of Thy sweetness and bid me enter. For with my heart and with my soul I do desire Thee, and I beseech Thee that Thou alone mayest possess me. Come, I am Thine, and Thou art mine; grant that with ever new fervor of spirit I may grow in living love for Thee, and blossom forth, by Thy grace, like the lilies of the valley near running water.

Then beseech the Virgin Mother, that she in her kindness may pray for thee:

O thou white lily, O thou who after God art my greatest hope, O most lovely Mary! Come, speak favorably of me to thy beloved Son; let thy speech be efficacious for me. Plead my cause faithfully. In thy mercy secure for me the object of my prayers, for I trust in thee, O thou who after Christ art my one and only hope!

Show plainly that thou art my gracious Mother. Intercede for me, that I may be received by the Lord in the cloister of love as in the school of the Holy Spirit—for there is no one more powerful than thou to obtain this from thy beloved Son. Mother most faithful, care for me, thy daughter, that I may become the fruit of ever living love, grow in all sanctity, and receive, like dew falling from heaven, the gift of perseverance.

Now invoke the grace of the Holy Spirit, that He may make thee advance in the monastic state:

Come, Holy Spirit, come, O Lord who art God, fill my heart, for alas! it is empty of anything good. Set me on fire, that I may love Thee. Enlighten me, that I may know Thee. Attract me, that I may delight in Thee. Arouse me, that I may experience the fruition of Thee.

Now separate thyself from the world and from anything whatsoever that is not thy dear love Jesus:

O most loving Jesus, Thou wilt give me wings like a dove, and I will fly forth in my desire of coming to rest in Thee.[1]

Now hide thyself in Jesus:

Come, dear Jesus, through the love wherewith Thou, being God, wast made man and camest to seek and to save that which was lost,[2] enter now, my Beloved, within me and grant me en-

[1] Cf. Ps. 54:7. [2] Cf. Luke 19:10.

trance likewise within Thee. Hide me in the immovable rock of Thy fatherly protection. In the cleft [3] of Thy most benign Heart, conceal me from all that is not Thyself, O Thou who art dearest of all things dear! And let my lot be cast among the people of Israel, that my portion may be with Thee among the daughters of Jerusalem. Amen.

Now cast thyself prostrate at the feet of Jesus:

Bless me, O most loving Jesus, and be merciful unto me according to the compassion of Thy most benign Heart. Oh, that my soul may choose to know nothing save Thee alone! Under the discipline of Thy grace and thanks to that anointing which teacheth all things, let me advance with ardor and rapidity in the school of Thy love.

At the moment when, in spirit, thou art clothed with the monastic habit:

O Father most holy, in that love whereby Thou hast signed me with the light of Thy countenance,[4] grant that I may advance towards Thee in all sanctity and virtue.

O Christ Jesus, in that love whereby Thou didst redeem me with Thy own blood, clothe me in the purity of Thy most innocent life.

O holy and almighty Paraclete, in that love whereby Thou hast sealed me for Thyself by a spiritual name, grant that I may love Thee with my whole heart, cleave unto Thee with my whole soul, expend all my strength in loving and serving Thee, live according to Thy Heart, and, at the hour of my death, enter immaculate upon the Divine nuptials made ready by Thee.

Beseech the Virgin Mother that she may be thy guide in the monastic state (or in whatever thy state of life may be):

O Mary, Mother of God, thou art also my most dear Mother!

[3] Cf. Cant. 2:14.   [4] Cf. Ps. 4:7.

Clothe me thyself with the fleece of the true Lamb, Jesus who was born of thee. Through thee may He who is supreme Love receive me, nourish me, possess me, shepherd me, and perfect me. Amen.

Now offer thy vow of chastity unto thy heavenly Bridegroom:

O dearest Jesus, I have made choice of Thee and Thee alone for my soul's faithful Lover, that I may live my life in Thy august companionship. For Thee doth my soul languish. I offer Thee the love of my heart; I choose Thee as my Betrothed and my guide. I offer my body and soul for Thy service, because I am Thine own, and Thou art mine.

Come then, O Love most true, unite me intimately unto Thee. I offer Thee my chastity, because Thou art all sweet and lovely, a Bridegroom full of delights. I vow obedience unto Thee, because Thy fatherly charity draweth me and Thy compassion and sweetness attract me; I pledge myself to do Thy will, because union with Thee outshineth the loveliness of all things else, and love of Thee is exceedingly sweet and desirable.

O Thou sole Beloved of my heart, I offer myself unto Thee, that henceforth I may live for Thee alone; for I have not found anything sweeter, or esteemed anything more profitable, than to be most intimately united with Thee.

Come, mould my heart after Thy own Heart, that I may deserve to be entirely pleasing unto Thee in my monastic observance.

RESPONSORY. The kingdom of the world and all earthly ornament have I despised, for love of my Lord Jesus Christ, whom I have seen, whom I have loved, in whom I have believed, whom I have loved exceedingly.

VERSE. My heart hath uttered a good word; wherefore I shall dedicate my deeds unto the King,[5] whom I have seen, whom I

5 Ps. 44:2.

have loved, in whom I have believed, whom I have loved exceedingly.

RESPONSORY. O Christ, true author and guardian of purity, who wast born of a Virgin and hast kindled the holy love of chastity in all who possess it, do Thou who art the virgins' exemplar, hope, and crown, keep me, through the intercession of Mary Thy Virgin Mother, chaste of mind and body.

VERSE. Thou art the fount of life and the source of perpetual light; Thou art the blessed author of all goodness.

PRAYER

Almighty and everlasting God, listen favorably to our prayers and bestow upon us Thy servants, who in the union of a common charity and for the honor of Thy name are here assembled, upright faith, unshaken hope, true humility, holy devotion, and perfect charity, together with zeal, constancy, and perseverance in good works. And through the merits and intercession of all the saints, graciously fill our hearts with a guileless love, strong patience, religion pure and undefiled, obedience well-pleasing unto Thee, enduring peace, purity of mind, holiness of conscience, compunction of spirit, strength of soul, spotlessness of life, and perfection without reproach, that we may run manfully and deserve the happiness of entering into Thy kingdom. Amen.

3rd Exercise

ESPOUSALS AND CONSECRATION

Commentary

THE RITE of the consecration of virgins, which is the liturgical background of the third Exercise, has a venerable history; it existed in the early fourth century, when the Church emerged from the catacombs. At that time the Christian women who had vowed their virginity to God, after being submitted to a long trial of their holy intent, were granted the distinction of being veiled, publicly and at Mass, by their bishop (or even by the Pope himself) and set apart for ever, by a solemn prayer of consecration, as the virginal brides of Christ. With the development of religious communities, this consecration gradually became the prerogative of cloistered nuns. As the ages went by, the ceremony was slowly amplified until by the end of the twelfth century it had grown into an elaborate ritual.[1]

It was a treasured memory of the nuns at Helfta that the first liturgical function ever performed in their abbey church was a ceremony of consecration. When the community left their former monastery at Rodarsdorf to take possession of the new buildings at Helfta in 1258, the Sunday next after the feast of the Holy Trinity was fixed for the singing of the first Mass. The "gracious and venerable" Archbishop Vulrad of Halberstadt, who had laid the cornerstone with his own hands, wished to welcome the nuns with all possible pomp and came in person to pontificate, surrounded by church dignitaries and

[27]

members of the nobility whose names have come down to us. On this occasion he consecrated several of the nuns according to the age-old ritual. These details have been preserved in the memorandum on the history of the community composed in 1451 by Sophia von Stolberg, who was then the ruling Abbess.[2]

Nuns of the Cistercian Order, it may be noted, did not receive the consecration. In the usages laid down for them by the General Chapter of Citeaux, the ancient rite had been replaced by a ceremony of profession practically identical with that of the monks of the Order; it was performed not by the bishop but by a Cistercian abbot.

The ceremony of consecration symbolizes the spiritual espousals of the soul with Christ the Divine Bridegroom. This latter experience, which belongs only to the highest degrees of the mystical life, was granted to Gertrude, not in a transient manner, but as that permanent awareness of the sacred alliance between God and the soul which is the state of the spiritual marriage.[3] This fact must be borne in mind if we are to understand the third Exercise in its true perspective.

The practice of renewing the consecration (for which this Exercise is intended) was familiar to both Gertrude and Saint Mechtild. We find in the *Herald* a chapter entitled: "The renewal of spiritual wedlock," which reads as follows:

> On Easter Tuesday, being about to receive Holy Communion again, Gertrude asked the Lord to deign to renew within her soul the spiritual wedlock whereby she had been espoused to Him in spirit, by her troth, her monastic way of life, and her untouched virginity.

This our Lord promised to do for her. He then imprinted a kiss on her soul, by which He renewed in her the inward exercise of her spirit; and under the symbolic form of a string of jewels, He gave her many graces, whereby He restored in her whatever she had lost by heedlessness in the spiritual exercises which she had labored to perform. The term used here for "spiritual wedlock" is *matrimonium spirituale*, the same as the *spirituale matrimonium* of the third Exercise.[4]

In the *Book of Special Grace* occurs a chapter with the heading: "How one may renew one's espousals." The word for "espousals," *desponsatio*, appears also in the title of the third Exercise. In this chapter we read that one day Mechtild reviewed in thought "all her years, and how heedlessly she had lived," and it seemed to her that "by her sins she had stained even her privilege of having been consecrated to God as His bride." Then she heard our Lord say to her,

> "If thou dost wish to renew thy espousals, come to My feet, giving thanks for the robe of innocence which I freely conferred on thee . . . Then in the smelting furnace of My Divine Heart, reshape the ring of thy troth and love, like gold tried in the furnace, and cleanse its stone in the water and blood of My Heart, that thence it may regain its value and beauty."[5]

On another occasion,

> she lamented to the Lord that she had neither solemnized the day of her espousals with proper devotion nor cleaved to Him with the fidelity that becomes a bride towards the one Bridegroom.[6]

The word used here for "solemnize," *celebrare*, appears at the head of not only the third but all the other Exercises with the exception of the fifth.

We do not know when either of our two saints had received her consecration. Since a candidate was not eligible for it before the age of twenty-five,[7] the earliest date for Mechtild would be 1266, five years after Gertrude's arrival at Helfta, and for Gertrude the earliest date would be 1281. According to the liturgical rubrics, the consecration could be given only on cer-

tain days; originally it was restricted to Epiphany, Easter week, and feasts of apostles; later on, feasts of our Lady and Sundays were added.[8] Now since Gertrude's twenty-fifth birthday occurred on the feast of the Epiphany, January 6, 1281, the interesting question suggests itself as to whether she may have been consecrated on that date. Her detailed written account of her spiritual life, starting with the event of January 27, 1281, is silent on this point,[9] which might seem to indicate that the ceremony had taken place earlier. On the other hand, the precise designation of "Easter Tuesday" in connection with the renewal of her espousals, which we have already quoted, may mean that it took place on the Easter Tuesday of that or of some later year, and that Gertrude simply refrained from mentioning it.

Gertrude's third Exercise is noted by the historians of the liturgy as showing indirectly how the rite was actually performed in her day.[10] For the reader's convenience, we have divided her prayers into groups by Roman numerals inserted in the text, to indicate how they correspond with the principal rites of the ceremony.

Part I is an introduction composed by Gertrude. Part II marks the beginning of the ceremony proper, which took place at Mass before the Gospel. By the antiphon, "Come ye! Come ye! Come ye, daughters, hearken unto me, and I will teach you the fear of the Lord," the bishop invited the chosen nuns to approach the altar.

Part III is a paraphrase of the litany of the saints and the thrice repeated verse, "Receive me, O Lord," which had passed from the Benedictine profession ceremony into the ritual of consecration.[11] The chosen nuns remained prostrate during the litany and the verse.

Part IV represents the essential part of the ceremony, being the prayer of consecration, which many authorities believe to have been originally composed by Pope Saint Leo the Great (d.

461). Saint Gertrude has transposed it from the third to the first person.

Part V refers to the investiture with the "insignia"—the veil, crown, and ring. The conferring of the veil, like the prayer of consecration, is essential to the rite; but the giving of the crown and the ring, and the singing by the chosen nuns of the exquisite antiphons from the office of Saint Agnes, were additions to the original ceremony which were made probably in the tenth century.[12]

It is recorded of Saint Hildegard (1098-1179) that she carefully preserved the crown which she had received on the day of her consecration.[13] The rite of crowning made a deep impression on Mechtild of Magdeburg, who must have witnessed it at Helfta; she has left us a prayer which she composed (in the vein of the psalm verse after the litany) on one such occasion:

> Receive, O Lord, Thy bride, and come every day to behold her with the lilies of pure chastity.
>
> Receive, O Lord, Thy bride, and come every day to visit her with the roses of diligent labor towards a happy death.
>
> Receive, O Lord, Thy bride, and come to visit her with the violets of lowly humility; lead her unto the couch of Thy nuptials, and unite her unto Thyself with all Thy love in a never-ending embrace.[14]

The flowers she mentions may have composed the garlands used as crowns.

The ring is spoken of in the passage already quoted from the *Book of Special Grace*; it is referred to early in the same book as being under the protection of our Lady.[15]

Part VI corresponds to the close of the ceremony. After the solemn blessing, the bishop recommends the chosen nuns to the care of their abbess;[16] Gertrude here asks our Lord, in the prelate's place, to present her to our Lady, to whom she now

[31]

lovingly gives the title of her "Abbess." The ceremony ends with the *Te Deum*.

Gertrude's prayer to the Trinity, Part VII, a lovely blending of humble gratitude and soaring praise, concludes this exercise in the atmosphere of heaven.

3rd Exercise

ESPOUSALS AND CONSECRATION

FOR THE ANNIVERSARY OF HOLY PROFESSION

This is the way in which thou shalt solemnize the spiritual wedlock, the marriage of love, the betrothal, and the nuptials of thy chaste soul with Jesus the heavenly Bridegroom in the deathless bond of thy heart's affection.

I

The voice of Christ to the soul:

Look upon Me and see who I am, O my dove;[1] I am Jesus, thy delightful friend. Open unto Me the secret places of thy heart. For I am from the land of the angels, and My beauty is beyond compare. I Myself am the brightness of the Divine Sun. I am that one most radiant day of spring which ever groweth clear and knoweth no twilight. The majesty of My superessential glory filleth both heaven and earth, and its amplitude is measured only by eternity. I alone wear upon My head the imperial diadem of My glorious Godhead. My brow is red with the blood which flowed for thee when it was pierced by the encircling thorns. Neither above nor beneath the sun is there anyone who is like unto Me.

[1] Cant. 2:10.

At the gesture of My hand, the lily-white choirs of virgins come forth. And I go on before them in the dance of eternal life, in the joyousness of My Godhead. I refresh them with the gladsome fruition of ever new delights. Nonetheless I do not disdain to lower My eyes unto the valley, out of which I may gather violets all unblemished.

She therefore who wisheth to give Me her heart's affection, she it is whom I will betroth unto Myself; unto her will I give My affection, and I will love her ardently. I will teach her the canticle of virgins, which resoundeth so melodiously from My lips that she will be constrained to unite herself unto Me in the delightsome bond of love. That which I am by nature, she shall be made by grace. I will embrace her in the arms of My love, pressing her unto the Heart of My Godhead, and thus by the strength of My burning love, she will melt away like wax from the face of the fire.[2] O My dove, My beloved, if thou dost wish to be Mine, thou must needs love Me sweetly, wisely, and strongly, that thou mayest experience these joys within thy soul.

Love awakeneth the soul:

Come, O soul, awake; how long wilt thou be slumbering? Hearken to the message which I bring thee. High above the heavens there is a King who is enthralled with desire of thee. He loveth thee with His whole Heart and loveth thee immoderately. He loveth thee so dearly, He loveth thee so faithfully, that for thy sake He humbly forsook His kingdom. While He was in quest of thee, He allowed Himself to be apprehended like a thief. He beareth thee such heartfelt love, His affection for thee is so ardent, He is so sweetly jealous for thee and drawn unto thee so fervently and powerfully, that He happily delivered up His beauteous body unto death for thy sake.

He it is who washed thee in His blood and saved thee by

2 Cant. 5:6; Ps. 67:3.

His death. How long must He wait before thou wilt love Him in return? He purchased thee and thy love at an exceeding great price. He hath had more affection for thee than for His own honor. He hath loved thee more than His own noble body, which He never spared for thy sake. This dear Love, therefore, this sweet Charity, this faithful Lover, doth require of thee thy love in exchange. If thou wilt accept this offer, He is ready to betroth thee unto Himself. Now therefore make haste to declare unto Him thy choice.

The voice of the soul offering herself unto God:

I am a motherless orphan; I am needy and poor. Apart from Jesus, I am devoid of all comfort. He alone can quench the thirst of my soul. He and He alone is the friend whom my heart chooseth rather than all others. He is the King of Kings and the Lord of Lords.[3] If He, supreme in His imperial sway, willeth to show His clemency unto me in my wretchedness and all my lowliness; if He willeth to deal with me according to His mercy and His infinite tenderness, this is the work of His bounty and resteth with His good pleasure. I am His by right. He holdeth my body and soul in His hand. May He do with me whatever shall be pleasing unto His goodness.

Oh who will grant my wish to be fashioned after His own Heart, that all His desires may be fulfilled in me according to His best good pleasure? Nothing but this can afford me joy and comfort.

Come then, O Jesus, Thou whom alone my heart loveth, Thou dear Lover, beloved, beloved, beloved above all that ever hath been loved! O Thou living flowery day of spring, the loving desire of my heart sigheth and fainteth after Thee. Oh would that it might befall me to be more closely united unto Thee, to the end that the flowers and fruits of my spiritual

---

[3] Apoc. 19:16.

progress may spring forth under the warmth of that true Sun which is Thou! Longingly I have awaited Thee.

Come then unto me like the turtle dove unto his mate. Thou hast wounded the secret places of my heart[4] by Thy comeliness and by Thy beauty. O my Beloved, if I attain not to be one with Thee, eternity can give me no joy. Come Thou, my Friend, my Friend, my Friend, effectively fulfil both Thy desire for me and mine for Thee.

The voice of Christ:

In My Holy Spirit I betroth thee unto Me, I take thee unto Myself in deathless union. Where I am, thou too shalt dwell; I will seclude thee within My living love. I will array thee in the noble purple of My precious blood. I will crown thee with the choice gold of My bitter death. Through Myself I will fulfil Thy desire, and thus I will make thee glad for evermore.

II

Now followeth the consecration, by which Christ's faithful soul doth consecrate, offer, and betroth her entire self unto the one Bridegroom, to present herself as a chaste virgin unto Christ,[5] being ready to cleave faithfully unto this same heavenly Bridegroom in the observance of virginity or chastity, with a pure heart, with a chaste body, and with bridal love which may never be defiled by an affection for any created thing. And first thou shalt sing the praises of the Bridegroom:

O Jesus Christ, my Lord and my dear Love, who is like unto Thee? Who, like Thee, is sublime and of limitless Being, and yet looketh with favor upon the lowly?[6] Among them who are strong, who is like unto Thee, O Lord, who dost choose the weak things of the world?[7] Who is such as Thou art, Thou who

---

4 Cf. Cant. 4:9. 5 Cf. 2 Cor. 11:2.
6 Cf. Ps. 112:6. 7 Cf. 1 Cor. 1:27.

didst create heaven and earth, who art served by the thrones and the dominations, who dost make it Thy delight to be with the children of men? [8]

What is Thy grandeur, O King of Kings and Lord of Lords,[9] who dost govern the stars and yet dost set Thy Heart upon man? [10] What is Thy nature, Thou who holdest riches and glory in Thy right hand? Thou art possessed of all delights, and wilt Thou take a bride of earth? Whither, O Love, dost Thou bow down Thy majesty? Indeed, O Love, Thou pourest the waters of the fountain of Thy wisdom into the very abyss of my wretchedness. O Love, Thine alone is this rich and overbrimming wine which doth master and inebriate my heart.

The proofs of Christ's love:

This is our God, who hath loved us with invincible love, with inestimable charity, and with deathless predilection. He assumed unto Himself the substance of a body of our earth in order that He Himself might become the Bridegroom and might take a bride. He hath loved us with His whole being, and the creature who loveth Him entereth into Divine nuptials with Him.

In remembrance of the bishop's words of invitation, "Come ye! Come ye! Come ye!"

I come, O most loving Jesus, I come unto Thee whom I have loved, whom I have sought, whom I have desired. Drawn by Thy kindness, Thy compassion, and Thy charity, I follow Thee, because Thou hast called me, and give Thee the love of my whole heart, and of my whole soul, and of my whole strength. Put me not to shame, but deal with me according to Thy clemency and the riches of Thy mercy.

III

Now recite this litany to invoke the help of all the saints:

[8] Cf. Prov. 8:31.   [9] 1 Tim. 6:15.   [10] Cf. Job 7:17.

LITANY

O most holy Trinity, one God, Thou fount of everlasting light, strengthen me by Thy Divine omnipotence, guide me by Thy Divine wisdom, and by Thy Divine bounty fashion me after Thy own Heart.

God, the Father of heaven and King of Kings, deign to wed me within my soul unto Christ the King, Thy Son.

Jesus, Son of the living God, let my love be wedded unto Thee, for Thou Thyself art my King and my God.

Holy Spirit, the Paraclete, join my heart for ever unto Jesus by that connecting tie of love wherein Thou dost unite the Father and the Son.

Holy Mary, Mother of the King, of the Lamb, of the Bridegroom of virgins, present me, pure in heart and body, for marriage with Jesus thy Son.

All ye holy angels and archangels, obtain entrance for me, in angelic purity, into the nuptial chamber of Jesus my Bridegroom.

All ye holy patriarchs and prophets, obtain for me the breadth and depth of charity which Jesus my Bridegroom doth require of me.

All ye holy apostles, pray that I may experience the kiss of His mouth,[11] of the glorious mouth of that living Word of God whom your hands have handled.[12]

All ye holy martyrs, obtain for me such a mighty desire to be, like you, a witness to the faith, that I may merit to bear the palm of martyrdom when I go forth to meet Him who weareth a crown of roses and lilies.

All ye holy confessors, secure for me this favor, that I may imitate in all perfection and holiness the virtues of Jesus my Bridegroom.

[11] Cf. Cant. 1:1.   [12] Cf. 1 John 1:1.

All ye holy virgins, pray for me, that by chaste love I may merit to build my nest like a turtledove in the wound of love in the Heart of Jesus my Bridegroom.

All ye saints, secure for me this favor, that I may be no less worthily prepared to enjoy the marriage of the Lamb, than one of your holy company to enjoy the vision of the face of God.

Be merciful and fashion me after Thy own Heart, O Lord.

Be merciful, and from aught that might hinder me from drawing near unto Thee, deliver me, O Lord.

Through Thy incarnation, make me love Thee sweetly, wisely, and strongly with my whole heart.

Through Thy passion and death, make me die unto myself and live unto Thee alone.

Through Thy glorious resurrection and wonderful ascension, make me daily advance from strength unto strength.

At the hour of my death, succor me with all Thy love and mercy, and give me gladness in the joy of Thy countenance, O Lord.

On doomsday let my soul fear not the hearing of condemnation, but do Thou cause me to hear Thy glorious voice pronouncing these words: "Come, ye blessed of My Father!" [13]

Through Thy most holy Mother, grant that I may be a true bride to enter upon the marriage of Thy chaste love.

We sinners, we beseech Thee, hear us.

That Thou wouldst deign to keep preciously for Thyself within me, unbroken and undefiled, the vow of chastity which I offer Thee: we beseech Thee, hear us.

That Thou wouldst make me experience, in bridal love and in Thy nuptial embrace, who and what Thou art: we beseech Thee, hear us.

That Thou wouldst bestow upon me the pledge of Thy Spirit

[13] Matt. 25:34.

[39]

with the whole and entire dowry of Thy love: we beseech Thee, hear us.

That at the hour of my death, in company with the wise virgins, Thou wouldst make me go forth as a bride, clad in the wedding garment and bearing my lamp alight, to meet that Bridegroom [14] who is Thyself: we beseech Thee, hear us.

That by the kiss of Thy glorious mouth, Thou wouldst bring me, as one who is wholly Thine, into the bridechamber of Thy dear love: we beseech Thee, hear us.

That Thou wouldst cause all of us who serve Thee in this place to love Thee wholeheartedly, cleave unto Thee by a deathless bond, and please Thee evermore by our purity of soul and body: we beseech Thee, hear us.

That Thou wouldst make us ask for what it is Thy good pleasure to grant: we beseech Thee, hear us.

Jesus, Son of the living God, graciously hear us in the omnipotence of Thy Divine love.

Lamb of God, who takest away the sins of the world, blot out all my sins according to the riches of Thy mercy.

Lamb of God, who takest away the sins of the world, atone for all my heedlessness by Thy charity whose fire can never be quenched.

Lamb of God, who takest away the sins of the world, at the hour of my death let me so depart in peace that I may see Thee face to face.[15]

Lord, be merciful unto us.

Christ, be merciful unto us.

Lord, be merciful unto us.

PRAYER

O Jesus, Thou Bridegroom who art like unto the flower of the field,[16] as death carrieth away soul from body, so may Thy

---

[14] See Matt. 22:11-12; 25:6, 10.   [15] Cf. Luke 2:29; 1 Cor. 13:12.
[16] See Cant. 2:1.

love carry away my heart into Thee, that by a deathless bond
I may cleave unto Thee.

Receive me, O my Jesus, into the abyss of Thy mercy, and
wash me from every stain in the depths of Thy clemency.

Receive me, O my Jesus, into the embrace of all the graces
Thou dost impart, that I may merit the nuptials of perfect
union with Thee.

Receive me, O my Jesus, into the dearest marriage of Thy
love; and make me experience therein the kiss of Thy glorious
mouth.[17]

IV

PRAYER

FOR PERFECT CHASTITY OF SOUL AND BODY

O God, who in Thy gracious kindness dost make chaste
bodies and pure souls Thy dwelling place! Thou, O God, when
human nature had been corrupted in our first parents by the
deceit of the devil, didst restore it by Thy Word, through whom
all things were made. Yet more, this nature of ours Thou hast
not only recalled unto its original innocence, but even uplifted
unto the experience of certain blessings which rightly belong to
the new age, already conferring upon men who formerly were
subject to the conditions of human life, a likeness unto the
angels.

Look with favor upon me, Thy unworthy handmaid, as I
place in Thy hands my vow of chastity; this dedication of myself I offer unto Thee, from whom I have received the very
desire which I do offer.

For how could our soul, being encased in mortal flesh, overcome the law of nature, licentious liberty, the force of custom,
and the urge of youth, if Thou didst not, through our free will,
kindle within us this love of chastity, nourish this desire in our

[17] Cf. Cant. 1:1.

hearts, and give us the strength to accomplish it? Thou hast indeed poured forth Thy grace upon all peoples and hast adopted, out of every nation under heaven, heirs of the New Testament as countless as the stars. And amongst the other virtues which Thou hast imparted unto Thy children (who are born not of blood, nor of the will of the flesh,[18] but of Thy Spirit), one pre-eminent gift hath flowed from the fount of Thy liberality into certain souls. For while no prohibition lesseneth the honor of marriage, and the initial blessing ever remaineth upon holy matrimony, nonetheless some loftier souls are found who, turning aside from the conjugal union of man and wife, desire the mystery which lieth hid therein; and, without seeking to imitate that which is wrought in marriage, love what is signified thereby.

Blessed virginity hath known her Author and, in emulation of the purity of the angels, hath pledged herself unto the bride-chamber and unto the couch of Him who is the Son of perpetual virginity, as of perpetual virginity He is the Bridegroom.

Grant then, O Lord, the defence and guidance of Thy protection unto me who now implore Thy succor and yearn to be strengthened by Thy sacred blessing. The loftier our desires, the subtler are the snares which the old enemy deviseth; suffer him not, through any carelessness of my soul, to creep in, seeking to dim the lustre of the palm of perfect continence; let him not snatch from the state of chastity that which should rightly be found even in the life of widowhood.

Establish within me, O Lord, by the gift of Thy Spirit, prudent modesty, wise kindness, grave mildness, and chaste liberty. Let me wax fervent in charity and set my affections upon naught save Thee; let me live praiseworthily and yet have no appetite for praise. Let me glorify Thee in holiness of body and in purity of soul, prefer Thee in love, and serve Thee out

[18] John 1:13.

of love. Be Thou my honor, Thou my joy, Thou my delight, Thou my solace in sorrow, and Thou my counsel in doubt. Be Thou my defence in injury, my patience in tribulation, my wealth in poverty, my sustenance in fasting, my slumber in watching, and my healing in sickness.

Let me have all things in Thee, whom I am eager to love above all things, and let me keep the vows of which I have made profession. O Thou who art the searcher of hearts, let me seek to be pleasing unto Thee rather in heart than in body. Then I shall be numbered amongst the wise maids and await the heavenly Bridegroom with lamp alight and oil prepared. Undismayed by the sudden advent of the King, I shall go forth in the train of the virgin choir to meet Him, rejoicing in the sure light of my lamp. I shall not be barred out with the foolish virgins but, with the wise, freely enter the royal courts, endure in chastity, and abide in the company of Thy Lamb in blessedness for evermore.

V

At the moment when, in spirit, thou dost take the veil:

RESPONSORY. The Lord hath clad me with the garment of salvation and girt me with the robe of happiness; and He hath adorned me like a bride with a crown.

VERSE. The Lord hath clad me with a dress woven of gold and set me off with countless jewels. And He hath adorned me like a bride with a crown.

PRAYER

Come, O my Beloved, chosen from among thousands, make me repose beneath the shadow of Thy charity and spread round about me, like a fleece, Thy spotlessness. There let me receive from Thy hand the veil of purity, and, under Thy tutelage and Thy guidance, may I present it unstained before the judgment seat of Thy glory, with the fruit a hundredfold of chastity and perfect innocence.

When, in spirit, the crown is placed upon thy head:

ANTIPHON. He hath put a mark upon my face, that I may admit no lover other than Himself.

RESPONSORY. Christ do I love, and I have entered the bride-chamber of Him whose Mother is a virgin and whose Father knoweth no woman, whose voice I hear singing in harmonious strains. If I love Him, I am chaste; if I touch Him, I am pure; and if I bid Him welcome, I am a virgin.

VERSE. Honey and milk have I received from out His mouth, and His blood hath adorned my cheeks. If I love Him, I am chaste; if I touch Him, I am pure; and if I bid Him welcome, I am a virgin.

PRAYER

Come, O Jesus, Thou my Brother,[19] Thou my Bridegroom, Thou great King, Thou who art God, Thou who art the Lamb! Put such a mark upon the face of my soul that I may choose nothing under the sun, desire nothing, love nothing other than Thyself. And do Thou Thyself, who art dearest of all things dear, deign so to take me unto Thyself in the bonds of mystical marriage, that I may be made Thy true bride and Thy true betrothed, by an indissoluble love stronger than death.[20]

When, in spirit, thou receivest the ring:

ANTIPHON. His ring He hath given me in pledge, He who far surpasseth all mankind in noble lineage and in grandeur.

RESPONSORY. His Body hath already passed my lips, and His Blood hath adorned my cheeks, whose Mother is a virgin and whose Father knoweth no woman.

[19] Cf. Cant. 8:1.   [20] Cf. *ibid.* 8:6.

VERSE. I am wedded unto Him whom the angels serve, at whose beauty the sun and moon do wonder.

PRAYER

O my Jesus, Thou fruit and flower of virginal purity, Thou best part of my inheritance, Thou my royal dowry, who hast given me in pledge the ring of Thy troth, the seal of Thy Spirit, come, make me all that I should be for Thee, my living Lily, my all-lovely Flower! Unite me so enduringly unto Thy all-burning love, that I may thirst for death in my eager desire to be with Thee; and let the marriage contract whereupon Thou hast entered with me so steal from me my heart, that it may be with me no longer but abide with Thee in a union of deathless love.

RESPONSORY. The kingdom of the world and all earthly ornament have I despised, for love of my Lord Jesus Christ, whom I have seen, whom I have loved, in whom I have believed, whom I have loved exceedingly.

VERSE. My heart hath uttered a good word; wherefore I shall dedicate my deeds unto the King, whom I have seen, whom I have loved, in whom I have believed, whom I have loved exceedingly.

PRAYER

Grant, I beseech Thee, O God Almighty, that I Thy unworthy handmaid who, for the hope of eternal reward, do desire to be consecrated unto Thee, may persevere in my holy vow with fulness of faith and constancy of soul. O Father Almighty, deign to hallow, and to bless, and to consecrate me for ever. Bestow upon me humility, chastity, obedience, charity, and abundance of all good works. For my works, O Lord, grant me glory; for my modesty, favor; and for my purity, holiness; that I may praise Thy most glorious majesty in company with Thy holy angels for all eternity. Amen.

VI

In remembrance of the blessing conferred by the bishop, beg that thou mayest be blessed by the whole gloriously reigning Trinity:

May the Divine majesty and the loving Paternity of God the Father bless me and grant me His cooperating grace. May the loving affinity and the consanguinity in human brotherhood of Jesus Christ, the Son of God, bless me and join me unto Him in marriage. May the loving benevolence of the Holy Spirit and His burning charity bless me and grant me fruitfulness. May the whole gloriously reigning Trinity bless, confirm, and strengthen me.

May the glorious manhood of Jesus Christ, the Son of God, bless me and receive me into union with Him, with Him who deigned to choose me out of the world unto Himself, who proved by His death His surpassing affection for me, and who hath made me the bride of His love. Thus by His saving, life-giving, and most loving blessing, may I obtain the perfection of all the virtues; may I keep whole and unspotted the chastity which I have professed, remain steadfast in my vow, give proof of humility, love chastity, hold fast to patience, and persevere unto the end in all holiness. And after this life may I deserve to receive the white robe and the crown of chastity amid the dazzling ranks of the pure, following Thee whithersoever Thou goest, O Thou spotless Lamb, Thou Son of the Virgin Mary, Thou flower of virgins! Amen.

Here pray the merciful Lord to recommend thee and entrust thee to His Mother, the all-pure Virgin Mary, as thy Abbess; and one day to receive thee back again from her hand.

O Jesus, Thou well-beloved of all my desires, Thou dearest of all most dear, entrust me now and recommend me to Thy

Mother, that virginal and queenly rose, that for love of Thee
she may ever be the mistress and protectress of my virginity.
Entrust me to her gentle hands which nourished Thee and
brought Thee up, Son of God the Father as Thou art, that these
same hands may defend me and succor me in the fulfilment of
my vow of chastity, guiding me without stain along the path of
virginal purity, or religious continence. Yea, speak to that virginal rose in my behalf and say: "Take this daughter under thy
motherly care; I recommend her to thee in full virtue of My
Divine charity. See to it, O Mother, that thou present her unto
Me again immaculate, and that thou restore her unto Me
fashioned after My own Heart." Amen.

*Now sing the hymn of thanksgiving in praise of the ever-
adorable Trinity:*

HYMN

Thee, O God, do we praise; we confess Thee to be the Lord.
Thee, the eternal Father, all the earth doth worship.
Unto Thee all the angels cry aloud, unto Thee the heavens
and all the powers,
Unto Thee the cherubim and seraphim continually do cry:
"Holy, Holy, Holy Lord God of hosts!
"Heaven and earth are full of the majesty of Thy glory!"
Thee do the glorious choir of the apostles praise,
Thee do the goodly company of the prophets praise,
Thee do the white robed army of the martyrs praise;
Thee doth holy Church throughout the whole world confess,
The Father of infinite majesty,
Thy adorable, true, and only Son,
Together with the Holy Spirit, the Comforter.
Thou art the King of glory, O Christ!
Thou art the everlasting Son of the Father.
Thou, when Thou tookest upon Thee to deliver man, didst
not abhor the Virgin's womb.

[47]

Thou, when Thou hadst overcome the sting of death, didst open the kingdom of heaven unto all who believe.

Thou sittest at the right hand of God, in the glory of the Father.

We believe that Thou art the Judge who is to come.

Thee we beseech, therefore, to help Thy servants, whom Thou hast redeemed with Thy precious blood.

Cause them to be numbered amongst Thy saints in eternal glory.

Save Thy people, O Lord, and bless Thy inheritance;

And govern them and raise them up for ever.

Day by day we bless Thee,

And we praise Thy name for ever and ever.

Deign, O Lord, to keep us this day without sin.

Be merciful unto us, O Lord, be merciful unto us.

Let Thy mercy, O Lord, be upon us, as we have hoped in Thee.

In Thee, O Lord, have I hoped: let me never be put to shame.

VII

PRAYER

O most holy Trinity, wherein shineth forth the living Deity, love, and wisdom; O Father, from whom all power doth take its rise, to whom Wisdom is coessential, and from whom floweth forth diffusive sweetness, flaming charity, radiant holiness, and all-pervading bounty—to Thee be praise, honor, and glory, to Thee be thanksgiving, power, and renown!

O Word, Thou who art the sublime cedar of Libanus, Thou, the regal majesty of whose Godhead resteth upon the cherubim, hast been pleased to bend down unto our lowly vale of tears and take unto Thyself this little sprig of hyssop in the nuptial embrace and in bridal love.

And Thou, O Holy Spirit, Love who art God, Thou loving

bond of union of the Holy Trinity, Thou dost rest among the children of men, taking Thy delight in holy purity which, in the strength of Thy love and Thy holy joys, gloweth like a rose shut in among thorns.

O Spirit of love, what road shall I follow to reach such happiness? What approach will bring me unto these spiritual joys? Where is the way of life leading unto these meadows whereon God Himself descendeth like dew for the refreshment of thirsting hearts? O Love! Thou alone knowest these paths of life and truth. In Thee the precious nuptial alliance with the Holy Trinity is accorded unto chosen souls. Through Thee the lofty charisms of the Spirit are bestowed.[21] From Thee proceed in all abundance the richest seeds of the fruits of life. Out of Thee floweth forth the indescribable sweetness of God's delights. Down from Thee distilleth the marvellous dewfall[22] of the blessings of the Lord of hosts, those precious pledges of the Spirit, which on our poor earth, alas! are so seldom found.

O Son of God, O Love, in Thy fair love[23] prepare for me the way which will lead me unto Thee; may I in chaste charity follow Thee eternally whithersoever Thou goest, in the love of Thy nuptial alliance with me, where Thou reignest and rulest in the infinite fulness of Thy Divine majesty! There, in the incomparable nuptials of Thy living love and in the living affection of Thy fiery Godhead, Thou dost lead after Thee in blessed heavenly ranks, the dazzling thousand times thousands of virgins, all adorned like Thyself in the same white garment and jubilantly singing the sweet canticles of the never-ending nuptials. Come then, O Love, keep me during this wretched life under the shadow of Thy charity; and after this exile bring me, spotlessly pure, amid that virginal band, into Thy sanctuary. There may the fountain of Thy Divine love be my sole refreshment and the enjoyment of Thyself my sole satisfaction. Amen! And let all things that have being say: Amen!

[21] 1 Cor. 12:31.   [22] Ps. 71:6.   [23] Cf. Ecclus. 24:24.

4th Exercise

RENEWAL OF MONASTIC PROFESSION

Commentary

SAINT Mechtild's charity, we are told, impelled her to remember in her prayers everyone in the abbey, including the novices, for whom "she begged that our Lord would confirm them in their profession of the monastic state and in true holiness."[1] Happily for us, the account of these prayers also includes some indications about the form of profession ceremony used at Helfta, without which we would be hard put to it to follow Saint Gertrude through the fourth Exercise.

In the *Book of Special Grace* we read:

> On the day of the novices' profession, when she was praying for them once more, . . . as the litany was being sung for them, she beheld [in a vision] the Blessed Virgin and then each saint, at the mention of his or her name, kneel down reverently to pray for them to our Lord. And while the novices were making their profession, the Lord Jesus took them most lovingly in His arms, holding out His right hand to each of them to help her in her vow and protect her from every kind of harm. When they came up for Communion, He favored each of them with a kiss, whereby she was given [the grace of] blessed union with Him.[2]

A shorter passage, which occurs in a different context—Mechtild was speaking of the sins which a nun might have the misfortune to commit—supplies another indication:

By transgressing obedience, she has, as it were, forsaken the yoke of the monastic state, of which she made profession to God in the presence of the saints.[3]

By comparing these details with the ceremonial of the profession of monks, which is based on the prescriptions in the Rule of Saint Benedict,[4] we shall be able to trace the ceremony well enough to understand the significance of the prayers which Gertrude has written for the renewal of monastic profession.

The prayers of Part I appear to refer to the request for the privilege of profession.

Part II is the invitation, with which we are already familiar from the third Exercise. Here, however, we have the detailed form of it. This rite is not peculiar to the consecration, but occurs in other liturgical ceremonies as well.[5]

Part III consists of four psalms and the litany, during all of which the novices about to be professed remained prostrate.[6] In her litany for the consecration, Gertrude has composed a series of invocations on the theme of the espousals of the soul with the Divine Bridegroom. In the present litany, everything centers on the making of the vows, and the themes are profession, monastic observance, and perseverance. The Blessed Virgin alone is named in the first litany; here, however, after the invocation to Mary, sixteen other saints are invoked by name, four of whom—Abraham, Moses, David, and George—do not appear in the official litany of the saints.

Part IV includes the act of profession; Saint Benedict requires, for the profession of monks, that the formula of vows should be drawn up in the names of the saints whose relics are kept in the church, as well as of the abbot, who must be present. This document must be written out in advance by the novice; his profession consists in reading it aloud before the altar, in the presence of the entire community, and then publicly signing it.[7] The acceptance of the yoke of the holy Rule, to which, as we have remarked, Saint Mechtild alludes as forming part of profession, is associated by Saint Gertrude with the thrice-repeated psalm verse already noted in the consecration ceremony. Here we have the verse in its original context, for it was from Saint Benedict's profession ceremony that it passed over into other rites.[8] The holy Rule prescribes that it should be sung by the new professed three times, obviously in honor of the Trinity, the monastic choir repeating it after him and adding the "Glory be to the Father" at the end. With this verse began the prostration at the feet of the community, also prescribed by the Rule.[9]

The cowl, or choir mantle, to which we find an allusion in the *Herald*,[10] the prerogative of the professed nun, is then conferred. The last sentence of Gertrude's prayer in Part V, "Come, O noble Love," contains the formula of presentation.

For the Communion of the new professed, Part VI, which Saint Mechtild describes so touchingly, Saint Gertrude has composed three exquisite prayers, which should be compared with those she gives in the first Exercise. These passages are especially interesting because of Gertrude's remarkable devotion to Holy Communion, so frequently expressed in the *Herald*. She tells us that her mystical life was intimately bound up with the reception of the Holy Eucharist.[11]

Two of the Gospel canticles, that of our Lady and that of Simeon, Gertrude takes as the theme of her thanksgiving, Part VII.

In all the editions of the *Exercises,* including the earliest, that of Lanspergius, the chapters follow the same sequence; yet one cannot help wondering why the Exercise on profession stands after, rather than before, the one on consecration, since in the order of time profession comes first? We have already noted that the consecration could not be received before the age of twenty-five, and presupposed that profession had taken place at some earlier date. Before the Council of Trent, the profession of nuns was allowed beginning with the age of twelve. We know that Saint Hildegard, who entered the pro-monastery of Saint Disibode as a pupil at the age of eight, was professed by the Bishop of Bamberg when she was fifteen;[12] but as for Gertrude, the date of her profession has not come down to us.[13] If she carried out her own rubric of renewing her consecration on the anniversary of her profession, it would appear from the passage we have already quoted that the latter ceremony occurred on an Easter Tuesday.

4th Exercise

RENEWAL OF MONASTIC PROFESSION

WHEN THE RELIGIOUS SOUL WISHETH TO RE-AWAKEN IN HERSELF THE GRACE OF HER DONATION

Thou shalt solemnize spiritually the renewal of thy profession or the desire of new fervor, with these most vehement desires and prayers, offering thy whole self to God as a burnt offering and a victim in the odor of sweetness.

I

O Father almighty, merciful, tender, and good, Thou who art exalted above human unfruitfulness, I call down Thy exceeding great mercy upon myself. Thou hast planted me in this most holy order, but I am like a little dried up branch; I have not, alas! observed the time of my pruning, but have passed the whole time of my life in great sterility. O Son of God, through Thy bounty, through the love of the Virgin Mary, Thy dearest Mother and our most glorious Patroness, and through the intercession of Saint Benedict, our venerable lawgiver, deign to turn upon me today the gaze of Thy mercy and of Thy charity. Thus shall I gain strength and grow all green again; I shall be sanctified in truth and burst into flower again; I shall become a faithful keeper of our holy monastic observance and a faith-

[57]

ful devotee of the spiritual life; and I shall bring forth unto Thee, who art my Lover, the fruits of all virtue and holiness, that at the time of grape gathering, that is, on the day of my death, I may be found in Thy sight fully ripe and consummate in all monastic perfection. Amen.

At the moment when, in spirit, thou receivest the blessing:

O my God, my Love most kind, may Thy divine omnipotence, wisdom, and bounty bless me and enable me to come after Thee with a most ready will, to deny myself in all truth, and to follow Thee most eagerly and most perfectly with my heart, spirit, and soul. Amen.

Now thou shalt invoke the grace of the Holy Spirit:

O my dearest Beloved! O my God, who art my mercy! Come, send forth now Thy Holy Spirit from heaven and create in me a new heart and a new spirit.[1] Let Thy anointing teach me concerning all things,[2] for I have chosen Thee out of thousands;[3] my affection for Thee surpasseth all other love, even the love of my own soul. May the strength of my soul be enriched by that beauty and loveliness of charity which Thou seekest, for I desire Thee ardently. Come, adorn me, that I may appear before Thee resplendently. Amen.

II

In remembrance of the bishop's words of invitation "Come ye!"

And behold, I come unto Thee whom I have loved, in whom I have believed, whom I have loved exceedingly.

PRAYER

O Thou who givest joy to my spirit, O Thou whom I praise with my heart and with my mouth, O my Jesus, I will follow

[1] Ezech. 18:31.   [2] Cf. 1 John 2:27.   [3] Cf. Cant. 5:10.

Thee whithersoever Thou goest! [4] Once Thou hast claimed my heart and taken possession of it as Thy own, Thou canst nevermore be taken away from me.

In remembrance of the second invitation, "Come ye!"

And behold, I come unto Thee whom I have loved, in whom I have believed, whom I have loved exceedingly.

PRAYER

O my Beloved, O my Jesus, I fold Thee unto my heart in the deathless embrace of charity. Behold, now that I have Thee within reach, I will hold Thee fast with all the love of my heart; even if Thou shouldst bless me a thousand times, I will never let Thee go again.[5]

In remembrance of the third invitation, "Come ye, daughters!"

And behold, I come unto Thee whom I have loved, in whom I have believed, whom I have loved exceedingly.

PRAYER

May all the power and strength of Thy Godhead praise Thee on my behalf; may all the love and affection of Thy Manhood make satisfaction to Thee in my behalf; may all the magnificence and ever-reigning majesty of the Trinity glorify and give honor unto Thyself, in Thyself, on my behalf, with that most sublime praise wherein Thou alone art sufficient unto Thyself and dost praise Thyself perfectly, filling up unto Thyself that which is wanting in all creatures.

In remembrance of these words of the same invitation, "Hearken unto me, I will teach you the fear of the Lord":

PRAYER

O Jesus, Thou good Shepherd, make me hear and know Thy

[4] Luke 9:57.   [5] Cf. Gen. 32:26.

[59]

voice. Lift me up in Thy arms. Let me rest in Thy bosom as Thy little ewe lamb to whom the Holy Spirit hath given fruitfulness; [6] there teach me the fear of Thee; there show me how I may love Thee; there make known unto me how I shall follow Thee. Amen.

III

Now recite Psalm 33:

I will bless the Lord at all times: His praise shall be always in my mouth.

In the Lord shall my soul be praised: let the meek hear and rejoice.

O magnify the Lord with me, and let us extol His name together.

I sought the Lord, and He heard me; and He delivered me from all my troubles.

Come ye to Him and be enlightened, and your faces shall not be confounded.

This poor man cried, and the Lord heard him and saved him out of all his troubles.

The angel of the Lord shall encamp round about them that fear Him and shall deliver them.

O taste, and see that the Lord is sweet! Blessed is the man that hopeth in Him.

Fear the Lord, all ye His saints, for there is no want to them that fear Him.

The rich have wanted, and have suffered hunger; but they that seek the Lord shall not be deprived of any good.

Come, children, hearken unto me; I will teach you the fear of the Lord.

Who is the man that desireth life, who loveth to see good days?

[6] See Isai. 40:11.

Keep thy tongue from evil, and thy lips from speaking guile.

Turn away from evil and do good; seek after peace and pursue it.

The eyes of the Lord are upon the just, and His ears unto their prayers.

But the countenance of the Lord is against them that do evil things, to cut off the remembrance of them from the earth.

The just cried, and the Lord heard them and delivered them out of all their troubles.

The Lord is nigh unto them that are of a contrite heart, and He will save the humble of spirit.

Many are the afflictions of the just; but out of them all will the Lord deliver them.

The Lord keepeth all their bones; not one of them shall be broken.

The death of the wicked is very evil, and they that hate the just shall be guilty.

The Lord will redeem the souls of His servants; and none of them that trust in Him shall offend.

ANTIPHON. Come ye unto Him and be enlightened, and your faces shall not be confounded.

PRAYER

O my God, Thou consuming fire, behold, I come unto Thee! Make me the prey of the mighty fire of Thy love, for I am only a little grain of dust; devour me and consume me utterly in Thyself. O Thou my dearest Light, behold, I come unto Thee! Enlighten me by the shining of Thy face, that my darkness may become as noontide in Thy presence. O Thou my Beatitude, behold, I come unto Thee! Unite me unto Thyself by the band of living love.

Now recite Psalm 23:

The earth is the Lord's and the fulness thereof, the world and all they that dwell therein.

For He hath founded it upon the seas and hath prepared it upon the rivers.

Who shall ascend into the mountain of the Lord? Or who shall stand in His holy place?

The innocent in hands and clean of heart, who hath not taken his soul in vain nor sworn deceitfully unto his neighbor.

He shall receive a blessing from the Lord and mercy from God his Saviour.

This is the generation of them that seek Him, of them that seek the face of the God of Jacob.

Lift up your gates, O ye princes, and be ye lifted up, O eternal gates; and the King of glory shall enter in.

Who is this King of glory? The Lord who is strong and mighty, the Lord mighty in battle.

Lift up your gates, O ye princes, and be ye lifted up, O eternal gates; and the King of glory shall enter in.

Who is this King of glory? The Lord of hosts, He is the King of glory.

ANTIPHON. This is the generation of them that seek the Lord, of them that seek the face of the God of Jacob.

PRAYER

O dearest Jesus, let me be enrolled and numbered in the generation of them that know Thee, O God of Israel; in the generation of them that seek Thy face, O God of Jacob; in the generation of them that love Thee, O God of hosts! Let me be so innocent in hands and so clean of heart, that I may receive a blessing and mercy from Thee, O God my Saviour.

Now recite Psalm 50:

Have mercy upon me, O God, according to Thy great mercy.

And according to the multitude of Thy tender mercies, blot out my iniquity.

Wash me yet more from my iniquity and cleanse me from my sin.

Unto Thee only have I sinned and have done evil before Thee; that Thou mayest be justified in Thy words and mayest overcome when Thou art judged.

For behold, I was conceived in iniquities, and in sins did my mother conceive me.

For behold, Thou hast loved truth; the uncertain and hidden things of Thy wisdom Thou hast made manifest unto me.

Thou shalt sprinkle me with hyssop, and I shall be cleansed; Thou shalt wash me, and I shall be made whiter than snow.

Unto my hearing Thou shalt give joy and gladness, and the bones that have been humbled shall rejoice.

Turn away Thy face from my sins and blot out all my iniquities.

Create a clean heart in me, O God, and renew a right spirit within me.

Cast me not away from Thy face and take not Thy Holy Spirit from me.

Restore unto me the joy of Thy salvation and strengthen me with a perfect spirit.

I will teach the unjust Thy ways, and the wicked shall be converted unto Thee.

Deliver me from blood, O God, Thou God of my salvation, and my tongue shall extol Thy justice.

O Lord, Thou wilt open my lips, and my mouth shall declare Thy praise.

For if Thou hadst desired sacrifice, I would indeed have given it; with burnt offerings Thou wilt not be delighted.

A sacrifice unto God is an afflicted spirit; a contrite and humbled heart, O God, Thou wilt not despise.

Deal favorably, O Lord, in Thy good will with Sion, that the walls of Jerusalem may be built up.

Then shalt Thou accept the sacrifice of justice, oblations, and whole burnt offerings; then shall they lay calves upon Thy altar.

[63]

ANTIPHON. Create a clean heart in me, O God; renew a right spirit within me.

PRAYER

Plunge me and immerse me in the abyss of Thy charity. Come, O Love, give freely; cleanse me from every stain in the laver of grace; and renew me, O Thou my true Life, in Thee.

Now recite Psalm 90:

He that dwelleth in the aid of the Most High, shall abide under the protection of the God of heaven.

He shall say unto the Lord: "Thou art my protector and my refuge; my God, in Him will I trust."

For He hath delivered me from the snare of the hunters and from the sharp word.

He will overshadow thee with His shoulders, and under His wings thou shalt trust.

His truth shall compass thee with a shield; thou shalt not be afraid of the terror of the night,

Of the arrow that flieth in the day, of the business that walketh about in the dark, of invasion, or of the noonday devil.

A thousand shall fall at thy side, and ten thousand at thy right hand; but it shall not come nigh thee.

But thou shalt consider with thy eyes and shalt see the reward of the wicked.

Because Thou, O Lord, art my hope; thou hast made the Most High thy refuge.

There shall no evil come unto thee, nor shall the scourge come near thy dwelling.

For He hath given His angels charge over thee, to keep thee in all thy ways.

In their hands they shall bear thee up, lest thou dash thy foot against a stone.

Thou shalt walk upon the asp and the basilisk, and thou shalt trample under foot the lion and the dragon.

Because he hoped in Me, I will deliver him; I will protect him because he hath known My name.

He shall cry unto Me, and I will hear him; I am with him in tribulation, I will deliver him, and I will glorify him.

I will fill him with length of days, and I will show him My salvation.

ANTIPHON. He that dwelleth in the aid of the Most High, shall abide under the protection of the God of heaven.

PRAYER

O Thou who art the protector of my soul and my refuge in the day of misfortune, overshadow me with Thy defending shoulders in every temptation and compass me with the shield of truth. Do Thou Thyself be with me in my tribulation; O Thou who art my hope, defend and protect me constantly from all dangers both of body and of soul. Come then, and after this exile show me Thyself, who art my dearest salvation. Amen.

LITANY

Lord, be merciful unto us.

Christ, be merciful unto us.

Lord, be merciful unto us.

Holy Trinity, who reignest undividedly, grant that my heart may fear Thee, love Thee exceedingly, and follow Thee, because I love Thee sincerely.

Holy Mary, paradise of sanctity and lily of purity, be thou the guide and guardian of my chastity, for in thee is all grace of life and of verity.

All ye holy angels and archangels, obtain for me devotedness in serving this King with my body and with my soul, according to His good pleasure, whom to serve is to reign, before whom you stand ministering without weariness and with ineffable joyfulness.

Saint John the Baptist, obtain for me illumination from the

brightness of that Light unto whom thou didst come to bear witness.[7]

O Father Abraham, obtain for me the faith and obedience through which thou wast the friend of the God of eternal existence.

O Moses, beloved of God, obtain for me that spirit of meekness, faith, and charity, which made thee worthy to speak face to face [8] with the God of majesty.

O David, thou venerable king and prophet, obtain for me that perfect fidelity, docility, and humility which made thee a man after God's own Heart,[9] wherefore in the sight of God the King thou wast pleasing in truth and set apart.

All ye patriarchs and prophets of holy mission, obtain for me the spirit of understanding and penetration.

Saint Peter, who dost hold the apostolic primacy, loose me from the bonds of all my sins by thy authority.

Saint Paul, thou vessel of election,[10] obtain for me the gift of veritable affection.

O my dearest John, thou disciple beloved of Jesus,[11] obtain for me the spirit of fidelity, purity, and holiness, for else I cannot please the Son of that Virgin, the Flower of that Lily whom thou didst guard with tenderness.

All ye holy apostles, whom Christ my Bridegroom called His friends and brethren, obtain for me union with Him by that charity which endureth even in heaven.

Saint Stephen, thou chosen protomartyr, obtain for me a keen desire to suffer martyrdom for Christ my Lover; and beg Him to be my helper who, in the hour of death, was unto thee a comforter.[12]

Saint Lawrence, thou soldier who didst never know defeat, obtain for me the love stronger than death whereby thou didst overcome the firebrand and the tormentor's wrath.

[7] Cf. John 1:7.   [8] Exod. 33:11.   [9] Cf. 1 Kings 13:14; Acts 13:22.
[10] Acts 9:15.   [11] John 13:23.   [12] See Acts 7:56.

Saint George, thou flower of martyrdom, obtain for me in God's service courage that shall not be overcome.

All ye holy martyrs, obtain for me patience and self-control, that I may be prompt for Jesus' love to lay down body and soul.

Saint Gregory, great apostle and shepherd of the sheep, obtain for me vigilance and perseverance in my holy monastic vows even unto death.

Saint Augustine, thou mirror of the Church, obtain for me to live my whole life for God and for the Church.

O Benedict, thou glorious founder of the monastic state, who art my father and one of God's chosen great, obtain for me in monastic observance such constancy that I may receive the crown of eternal life together with thee.

All ye holy confessors, obtain for me the raiment of beauty and praise,[13] that all my life and deeds may tell forth unto the Lord the mercies He hath shown in all His ways.

Catherine, thou who didst endure the wounding of God's love, thou saint so pure, obtain for me scorn of every earthly treasure and love of Jesus without measure.

Saint Agnes, thou youthful follower of the Lamb, obtain for me love of Jesus my Bridegroom and charity fire-tried, thou whose glory it was to yield unto His love, possess the pledge of His troth, and enter His nuptial chamber as His bride.

Saint Mary Magdalene, thou who wast Christ's most fervent lover, obtain for me all diligence in monastic observance, as its most faithful keeper.

All ye holy virgins and widows, obtain for me in the life of the spirit such progress that I may attain unto the goal of holiness.

All ye saints and elect of God, obtain for me in monastic observance such holiness that I, with you, may come unto that eternal blessedness where naught is experienced save joy and where God is all in all.[14]

[13] Cf. Ps. 95:6.   [14] Cf. 1 Cor. 15:28.

[67]

Be merciful unto my sins and all my heedlessness, and deign to atone for the errors of my corrupt way of life by Thy most perfect way of life, O Lord.

From timidity of spirit and from storminess, from all perversity of heart and from fleshliness, from all heedlessness in my behavior and from wickedness, deliver me, O Lord.

Through all the fatherly mercy of Thy Heart, grant me understanding and instruct me in this vow of holy religion (which I now pronounce before Thee); for I acknowledge that I am nothing, that I know nothing, and that I can do nothing without Thee.

Through Thy most holy Mother, lead me in the path of purity, that I may be pleasing unto Thee soul and body.

I, Thy unworthy and prodigal daughter (who, alas! by my sins have lost the name of daughter), trusting in Thy fatherly kindness, do entreat Thee: according to the multitude of Thy mercies, look upon me, blot out all my irreverence and undutifulness, and graciously hear me.

That Thou wouldst deign to grant me, in the holy monastic state, a spirit with the victor's crown, and a heart humbled and cast down; a mind most reverent, and a body most obedient: we beseech Thee, hear us.

That Thou wouldst deign to infuse into me the grace, relish, and love of the life of the spirit: we beseech Thee, hear us.

That Thou wouldst make me renounce the world completely and cleave unto Thee devotedly: we beseech Thee, hear us.

That Thou wouldst make me faithful in holy monastic observance and grant me therein perseverance: we beseech Thee, hear us.

That Thou wouldst deign to bestow upon all of us who serve Thee in this place, oneness of spirit in the bond of charity and of peace;[15] and that Thou wouldst deign to bring us, after this

[15] Eph. 4:3.

life, unto the reward of Thy glory which Thou hast promised us: we beseech Thee, hear us.

That Thou wouldst deign, by all the authority of Thy Godhead, to absolve me from all my sins and to strengthen me in my holy vows; and, by all the affection of Thy Manhood, to show Thyself favorable unto me and graciously to hear me in all these requests: we beseech Thee, hear us.

Jesus, Son of the living God, the reason of my desire is known unto Thee alone; fashion me after Thy own Heart: we beseech Thee, hear us.

Lamb of God, in this way wherein I walk, hold Thou my right hand lest I grow faint.

Lamb of God, make me faithfully fulfil that which I have undertaken in Thy name.

Lamb of God, let not my sins hold me fast, but let Thy mercy cause me to advance in all these things.

Christ, hear me and grant unto me in the hour of my death the joy of Thy salvation.

Lord, be merciful unto us.

Christ, be merciful unto us.

Lord, be merciful unto us.

PRAYER

O God, who with incomparable art dost plant and protect all the virtues, make me—who, in my unworthiness, am like the least seed of Thy true sowing—wax strong in my adherence unto the holy monastic state, grow in the fruits of the more perfect life a thousandfold, and persevere unto the end of my life, faithful and unwearied in Thy holy service.

IV

Invoke the Divine Wisdom to aid thee, reciting this responsory:

RESPONSORY. Send forth Wisdom, O Lord, from the throne of Thy majesty, that she may be with me and may labor with me; that I may know at all seasons what is acceptable in Thy sight.[16]

VERSE. Give unto me Wisdom, O Lord, that sitteth by Thy throne,[17] that I may know at all seasons what is acceptable in Thy sight.

Now shalt thou give unto the Lord the written bond of thy profession, saying:

O Jesus, my dearest Beloved, I wish to embrace with Thee the Rule of love, that I may renew my life and may spend it in Thee. Come, place my life under the care of Thy Holy Spirit, that at all seasons I may be most prompt to keep Thy commandments. Conform my behavior unto Thine; strengthen me in love of Thee and in peace. Surround my understanding with the light of Thy charity, that Thou alone mayest teach me, lead me, and instruct me in the secret places of my heart. Engulf my spirit in Thy Spirit so powerfully and so deeply that I may in truth be entirely buried in Thee, abandoning myself in union with Thee, and the place of my burial may be known unto Thy love alone. May this same love close my tomb under its seal and bind me unto Thee with a deathless bond. Amen.

Here turn thee unto the Lord and await the first obedience which His love shall lay upon thee:

My Beloved calleth unto me: "Put Me as a seal upon thy heart and upon thy arm, for love is strong as death." [18]

Make thyself ready most eagerly to enter with the Lord upon the way of fair love:

RESPONSORY. I will love Thee, O Lord, who art my strength; the Lord is my firmament, and my refuge, and my deliverer.

---

[16] Cf. Wisdom 9:10.   [17] *Ibid.* 9:4.   [18] Cant. 8:6.

VERSE. I will praise the Lord and call upon Him, and I shall be saved from my enemies. The Lord is my firmament, and my refuge, and my deliverer.[19]

Now take upon thee anew the yoke of the holy Rule:

Receive me, O Father most holy, in Thy all-clement Fatherhood, that at the end of this course of holy monastic observance (which, for love of Thee, I have undertaken to run), I may receive Thee Thyself as my crown and my eternal inheritance.[20]

Receive me, O Jesus most loving, in Thy bounteous Brotherhood, that Thou mayest bear with me all the burden of the heat of the day,[21] and I may have Thee as my comforter in all my labor and as my tutor, guide, and companion on my journey.

Receive me, O Holy Spirit, Love Divine, in Thy most compassionate mercy and charity, that I may have Thee as the master and instructor of my whole life, and the dearest Lover of my heart. Amen.

Here cast thyself prostrate before the Lord:

Lord, be merciful unto us.
Christ, be merciful unto us.
Lord, be merciful unto us.

Now recite once more Psalm 50, as thou didst at the beginning of this Exercise. And then say:

O most loving Father, I cast myself at Thy feet! Behold, my sins have set up a barrier between Thee and me. Come, be merciful unto me, according to the multitude of Thy tender mercies, and break asunder the wall of my past way of life, which withholdeth me from Thee; and draw me unto Thee so

---

[19] Cf. Ps. 17:1-4.   [20] See 1 Cor. 9:24.   [21] Cf. Matt. 20:12.

powerfully that, in the sweetness of Thy deathless love, I may follow Thee with affection and understanding.

PRAYER

Alas, most loving Jesus! Although the desire is in me, I cannot encompass it [22] because of the frailty of human nature. Succor me, therefore, by Thy grace, and convert my soul unto Thee by the all-pure law of Thy love, that running in the way of Thy commandments [23] without weariness and cleaving unto Thee without wavering, I may have Thee with me, my Lord, ever helping and strengthening me in the task which I have undertaken for love of Thy love.

V

Think then that thou art to receive the holy monastic cowl, and say this prayer:

Come, O noble Love, and cause me, ignoble reed that I am, to blossom like a lily at sight of Thee. The hand of Thy sublime Godhead did plant me in the deep valley of holy humility, beside the superabounding waters of Thy charity, beside the broad waters of Thy pardon and compassion. Come, O my sweet morning Sun, cause this dry straw that I am (planted by Thee, though of myself I am but naught), to grow all green again in the fulness of Thy Spirit and to flower again in Thee. Make me thus, in Thee, strip myself of the self with its deeds [24] and put on a new being, created according to God in justice and holiness of truth.[25] Amen.

RESPONSORY. The kingdom of the world and all earthly ornament have I despised, for love of my Lord Jesus Christ, whom I have seen, whom I have loved, in whom I have believed, whom I have loved exceedingly.

[22] Cf. Rom. 7:18.   [23] Cf. Ps. 118:32.   [24] Cf. Col. 3:9.
[25] Cf. Eph. 4:24.

what am I? Alas! I am but the least of all Thy creatures.[29] Yet Thou art my great confidence, for in Thee is laid up for me [30] enough to make up in richest abundance for all that I have lost. Come, O Love, O Love, O Love, heap upon me the vastness of Thy immense bounty and mercy. Load me and weigh me down with all Thy infinite compassion and clemency. Let me draw my last breath amid the breathing of Thy dearest Spirit and fall asleep beneath the veil of Thy love. While I yet live, let me give up the ghost at the taste of Thy sweetness, that passing out of myself into Thee, who art my dear delight, I may gently depart, fall into Thy embrace, and be most truly buried in the kiss of Thy ineffable love.

Wrap me in the winding sheet of Thy dear redemption. Embalm me in the perfume of Thy precious death. Lay me in the marble tomb of Thy Heart which was transpierced by the lance, hiding me beneath the stone of the gentle gaze of Thy most beauteous countenance, that Thou mayest watch over me for evermore. O my Beloved, let me be buried in the gracious shadow of Thy fatherly love. Let me rest, let me rest, let me rest in the everlasting memory of Thy precious and living affection. Come, O mighty Love, let my flesh wither away in Thee. O quickening Love, let my life breathe itself out in Thee. O clement Love, let my whole being be burned to ashes in Thee. And may my soul rest eternally in the ineffable light of Thy countenance. Amen.

VII

Then thou shalt recite in thanksgiving the canticle of our Lady (Luke 1:46-55):

My soul doth magnify the Lord, and my spirit hath rejoiced in God my Saviour,

Because He hath regarded the humility of His handmaid; for behold, from henceforth all generations shall call me blessed,

---

29 1 Cor. 4:13.   30 2 Tim. 4:8.

Because He that is mighty hath done great things unto me, and holy is His name.

And His mercy is from generation unto generations, unto them that fear Him.

He hath showed might in His arm; He hath scattered the proud in the conceit of their heart.

He hath put down the mighty from their seat and hath exalted the humble.

He hath filled the hungry with good things, and the rich He hath sent empty away.

He hath received Israel His servant, being mindful of His mercy,

As He spoke unto our fathers, unto Abraham, and unto his seed for ever.

Whereunto thou shalt add this prayer:

Unto Thee, O God of my life and Life-giver of my soul, unto Thee, my dearest Lover, Father, Bridegroom, and Providence, I present the entire treasure of my love, for the furnace of Thy fiery Spirit and for the blazing flames of Thy living love. For Thy sake, O Thou who art dearest of all things dear, at this hour I enter upon hard ways,[31] knowing that Thy mercy is more blessed than life itself.[32] Come, O my Beloved, I put my trust in Thy compassion! By Thy Divine power, gird me for war with the armor of Thy Spirit;[33] make me strong to overcome all the wiles of my enemies; and, by Thy ever-burning charity, do Thou Thyself overpower within me aught that liveth not utterly for Thee. Then I shall be drawn toward Thee and refreshed by the gentle assistance of Thy living love and the quickening sweetness of Thy affection, and I shall love Thee exceedingly. May I love Thee exceedingly, O Thou my sweet Strength, and joyfully follow after Thee bearing the sweet yoke and the light

[31] Ps. 16:4.   [32] Ps. 62:4.   [33] Cf. Ps. 17:40.

burden [34] of Thy love, that all the labor of the service which I undertake, O my Beloved, for Thee, may seem unto me but a few short days because of the greatness of my love.

May the cool refreshment of Thy Spirit shorten and lighten for me all the burden of the heat of the day.[35] Do Thou Thyself deign to intermix all the works and the exercises of my life with the works of the life of Thy living love, that my soul may magnify Thee eternally, my whole life serve Thee untiringly, and my spirit rejoice in Thee, O God my Saviour; and let all my thoughts and all my actions be offered unto Thee in praise and thanksgiving. Amen.

When thou hast said these prayers, commend thyself unto the Lord by the canticle of Simeon (Luke 2:29-32):

Now Thou dost release thy servant, O Lord, according to Thy word, in peace,

Because my eyes have seen Thy salvation,

Which Thou hast prepared before the face of all peoples:

A light unto the revelation of the Gentiles, and the glory of Thy people Israel.

And add this prayer:

Come, O Love, my King and my God, O Jesus my dearly Beloved, into the most tender care of Thy Divine Heart now receive me. There, that I may live for Thee alone, by Thy love retain me. Come, within the depths of the vast ocean of Thy mercy now release me. There, unto the love of Thy superabounding compassion entrust me. Come, in the devouring flame of Thy living love now immerse me. There, until my soul and spirit are burned unto ashes in Thee, transport me. Come, and at the hour of my death, unto the Providence of Thy fatherly charity, entrust me.

There, O my blessed Salvation, by the sight of Thy ineffable

---

[34] Cf. Matt. 11:30.   [35] Cf. *ibid.* 20:12.

presence console me. There, by the taste of that dear redemption wherewith Thou hast ransomed me, refresh me. There unto Thyself by the living voice of Thy fair love, call me; there into the embrace of Thy most loving and forgiving gentleness, receive me. There unto Thyself, in the delightsome breathing of Thy sweet-flowing Spirit, attract me, draw me, and consume me. There in the joy of eternal attainment of Thee, in the kiss of perfect union, immerse me; and grant then that I may behold Thee, that I may possess Thee, and that in eternal happiness I may enjoy Thee, for my soul desireth Thee, O Jesus, Thou who art dearest of all things dear! Amen.

5th Exercise

TO STIR UP THE LOVE OF GOD

Commentary

THE FIFTH Exercise, Saint Gertrude's "day of love," falls into two main parts. In Part I she addresses to our Lord a threefold series of prayers to be offered in the morning, at noon, and in the evening, each series being introduced by three psalm verses. The first series, where she gives our Lord the beautiful title of her "Morning," reminds one of her description of the early spring morning in 1281 when, during her prayer on the banks of the pond, she was given such a wonderful grace of spiritual enlightenment.[1]

In this same series we encounter some instances of a personification of Divine love which at first sight is somewhat disconcerting, since this love is styled a "queen," *regina,* or a "bride," *uxor, sponsa.* It is not uncommon, however, in medieval literature and art, to find the virtues represented as beautiful maidens; numerous instances occur in the *Book of Special Grace* and in *The Flowing Light of the Godhead.* And in some passages of the latter book, Mechtild of Magdeburg also refers to Divine love as a queen.[2] We shall see how Saint Gertrude makes elaborate use of the device of personification in the seventh Exercise.

In the third series, in which she addresses our Lord as her "Evening," she asks of Him "the heavenly kiss" that will make her die to herself. Here (and the same should be said of the passages we have already met with where she mentions our Lord's "kiss") she speaks the language not of earthly lovers but of the mystics, to whom the opening verse of the Canticle of Canticles, "Let Him kiss me with the kiss of His mouth," has always signified God's sublime manifestation of Himself in the mystical ways. Gertrude was familiar with the celebrated commentary on the Canticle by Saint Bernard; several quotations from this work are found in the *Herald*,[3] and one of these same excerpts —brief but striking—reappears in the sixth Exercise.[4] The eighth sermon of the commentary gives us some insight into Gertrude's meaning in the present instance. There Saint Bernard says that in the Holy Trinity, the mutual knowledge and love of the Father and the Son may be called Their kiss; this is incommunicable to any creature. The words "the kiss of His mouth," however, refer to the Holy Spirit, who proceeds from the Father and the Son. The bride of the Canticle, therefore, when she says, "Let Him kiss me with the kiss of His mouth," is asking that the Holy Spirit may be poured forth upon her. Through this outpouring, the soul of the mystic is enlightened with knowledge of the Trinity and enkindled with love for the three Divine Persons.[5] Some such experience as this is what Gertrude wishes to convey when she speaks of the "kiss."

In Part II, a sevenfold series of prayers is linked with the Hours of the Divine Office, reckoned thus: Matins, Prime, Terce, Sext, None, Vespers, and Compline. The introductory verses in this case are free compositions, with only slight reminiscences of Scripture here and there. The prayers are a free development of the idea of the "school of love" which was lightly touched on in the second Exercise.

The "alphabet" introduced under the hour of Terce is doubtless based on the name Christ gives Himself of "Alpha and Omega" (Apocalypse 1:8). Here again Abbot Emmanuel supplies a helpful explanation. He informs us that Gertrude uses "Alpha" for the beginning of the science of love; "Beta" (the second letter of the Greek alphabet), for progress in good works; "Tau" (the last letter of the Hebrew alphabet), for perfection; "Omega" (the last letter of the Greek alphabet), for supreme perfection. "Iota" has its usual sense.[6]

Saint Gertrude, as we know from at least two passages in the *Herald,* had received the mystical favor, accorded also to Saint Teresa of Avila three hundred years later, of the wound of love in her heart.[7] It is not surprising that in this Exercise devoted to love, she should allude to it; and in fact she does so twice. The first allusion appears in the prayer for the hour of Vespers. The phrase "Thy sharp arrows" (taken from Psalm 44:6) coincides perfectly with the narratives in the *Herald.* A new idea, however, is added—that the powerful current of infused love is a source of strength and confidence amid the temptations that beset the soul on her spiritual path. The second allusion, in the prayer for the hour of Compline, expresses the longing for death in order to be with God, which is another effect of the wound of love.

Part III, the conclusion of this Exercise, begins with a little series of "beatitudes," evidently suggested by the text, "Blessed are your eyes because they see, and your ears because they hear" (Matthew 13:16).

Finally, Gertrude prays for one of the highest graces of the interior life, that of confirmation in love. This grace means that, by God's gift, charity is tremendously increased in the soul of the person who receives it, turning him more and more completely away from sin. God's special protection is also necessary to maintain him in this state.[8] Confirmation in love is one of the fruits of the lofty degree of union with God in which Saint Gertrude lived during the greater part of her mystical life. Her keen awareness that all her gifts came not from any merit of hers but from God's bounty, led her to pray for it so humbly. We who are far from perfection may at least beg of God the great increase in humility and charity which it is His will to give us.

5th Exercise

TO STIR UP THE LOVE OF GOD

I

Whenever thou dost wish to give thyself up to love, thou shalt withdraw thy heart from all inordinate affections, hindrances, and useless images. Choose thee a day for this exercise and a time which will be fitting—at least three hours of that day, one in the morning, one at noontide, and one in the evening—in atonement for never having loved the Lord thy God with thy whole heart, with thy whole soul, and with thy whole strength. Then thou shalt unite thyself in prayer unto God, with all thy affection and devotion and with a pure intention, as if thou didst behold present before thee Jesus thy Bridegroom, who is assuredly present in thy soul.

1

In the morning, as if thou wert going forth to meet thy God, recite these three verses from Psalm 62:

O God, my God! unto Thee do I watch at break of day.

For Thee my soul hath thirsted; for Thee my flesh, oh in how many ways!

In a desert land, and where there is no way and no water; so in the sanctuary have I come before Thee, to see Thy power and Thy glory.

Then add the following prayer:

Come, O Love, O God, Thou alone art all my love in verity. Thou art my dearest Salvation, all my hope and my joy, my supreme and surpassing Good. In the morning I will stand before Thee, my God, and will contemplate Thee,[1] my dearest Love, because Thou art pure delightsomeness and sweetness eternal. Thou art the thirst of my heart; Thou art all the sufficiency of my spirit. The more I taste Thee, the more I hunger; the more I drink, the more I thirst.

Unto me, O Love, O God, the vision of Thee is day most radiant, that one day in Thy courts which is better than a thousand[2] elsewhere, that one day after which sigheth this soul of mine redeemed unto Thyself by Thee. Come, when wilt Thou satisfy me with the sweetness of Thy glorious face? My soul longeth and fainteth[3] after the richness of Thy delights. Behold, I have chosen and preferred to be a poor handmaid in the house of my God,[2] that I may approach unto the refreshment of Thy all-beauteous face.

O Love, to behold Thee is to fall into an ecstasy in God. To cleave unto Thee, is to be joined unto God in spiritual marriage. O Thou most serene Light of my soul and most radiant Morning, come, shed within me the rays of Thy dawn, and so enlighten me that in Thy Light I may see light,[4] and through Thee my night may be turned into day. O my dearest Morning, for love of Thy love let me count as naught and as vanity all that Thou art not. Come, visit me now early in the morning,[5] that in a moment I may be wholly transformed into Thee.

O Love, who dost not clarify but deify, come now unto me generously, that through Thee I may melt away lovingly; let me

[1] Cf. Ps. 5:5. [2] Cf. Ps. 83:11. [3] Ps. 83:3.
[4] Cf. Ps. 35:10. [5] Cf. Job 7:18.

die unto myself and pass into Thee unreservedly, nor ever have power to turn back unto myself momentarily, but rest united unto Thee eternally.

O Love, Thou art that Unity, that foremost Beauty, who in this world art not seen save from beneath the wings of the seraphim. Oh when wilt Thou refresh me with Thy surpassing beauteousness? O morning star[6] who ever reignest, resplendent with Divine brightness! Oh when shall I behold Thy presence in its loveliness?

O Splendor who callest forth all love, when wilt Thou grant me to attain Thee? Oh that here I might perceive the delicate rays of Thy beauty for a moment, that I might have at least a foretaste of Thy sweetness for an instant, and sweetly anticipate the joy of possessing Thee as my best part! Now turn Thee towards me a little, that I may fix my gaze upon Thee, O Thou Flower of flowers.

Thou art the glorious mirror of the Most Holy Trinity, into which the eyes of the clean of heart may gaze, here only darkly, but there face to face. Come, sprinkle me over with Thy purity, and I shall be cleansed. Touch the secret places of my heart with Thy cleanness, and I shall be made whiter than snow. Let Thy charity, I beseech Thee, prevail by its greatness, and let Thy merits infold me with their abundant holiness, lest I be held back from Thy beauty by my unlikeness.

Look upon me and behold me, and make me acknowledge Thee and know Thee. Thou hast first loved me. Thou hast chosen me, whereas I had not chosen Thee.[7] Of Thy own accord Thou goest forth to meet the soul who thirsteth for Thee; upon Thy brow shineth the splendor of eternal light.

Come, show me Thy face and make me contemplate Thy loveliness. Yea, Thy face is winning and beautiful, radiant with the fairest dawn of the Godhead. In the color of Thy cheeks is written in red the wondrous name Alpha and Omega.[8] In Thy

---

[6] Cf. Apoc. 22:16.   [7] Cf. John 15:16.   [8] Apoc. 1:8.

eyes burneth the deathless glory of eternity; their light is unto me the lamp of the salvation of God. In Thee the beauty of charity doth enhance the splendor of truth. The fragrance of life breatheth forth unto me from Thee. Honey and milk[9] come unto me, drop by drop, from Thy mouth.

How beautiful art thou, O CHARITY who art God! How lovely, how wonderful, how admirable thou art in thy incomparable delights! Thou art the queen who dost sit first upon the Divine throne; the fulness of the riches of the ever-reigning Trinity is thine. Thou dwellest ever in the house of God most high as His betrothed and His bride; thou art united unto the Son of God in deathless love.

O LOVE, at the sunset of my life, deign thou to rise for me early in the morning, and when thou seest me about to leave this my dwellingplace, open unto me the source of eternal life which is in thee; and grant me so to finish with this my exile, that I may go in with thee unhindered unto the marriage of the Lamb,[10] find, with thy help, the true Bridegroom and Beloved, and be so closely united unto Him in thy arms that I may nevermore be separated from His embrace.

Then, O Love, O Key of David,[11] do Thou unlock and open unto me the holy of holies, that given entrance by Thee I may not tarry, but joyfully behold in Sion that God of gods[12] whose glorious countenance my soul now desireth and greatly longeth for.

2

At noontide, draw near unto thy Bridegroom who burneth with love for thee, that He, the Sun of Justice, may enkindle thy lukewarmness by the noontide heat of His love, until the glowing coals of Divine love never cease to burn upon the altar of thy heart. And first recite these verses from

[9] Cant. 4:11.
[11] Cf. *ibid.* 3:7.
[10] See Apoc. 19:7, 9.
[12] Cf. Ps. 83:8.

Psalm 17:

I will love Thee, O Lord, my strength.

My God is my helper.

My Protector, and the Horn of my salvation.

Then add this prayer:

Come, O Love, Thou first flower of my love, Thou art the most precious pledge of my bridals, Thou art my marriage portion. Behold, for Thy sake I have scorned the world, and I have counted all earthly joy as dust beneath my feet that I might aspire to be wedded unto Thee.

Come, admit me unto the intimacy of Thy charity. Behold, my heart burneth already for the kiss[13] of Thy love. Open unto me the privy chamber of Thy fair love. Behold, my soul thirsteth for the embrace of most secret union with Thee.

Come, now prepare the banquet of Thy rich mercy, inviting me unto the table of Thy delights. Set before me the delectable dish of Thy eternal merciful forgiveness, which alone can give strength unto my spirit.

Come, now let us feast together, O my dearest, my supreme Good! Thou dost abound in Thyself with all blessings, yea, Thou dost overflow with goodness beyond all reckoning, and, oh marvel! Thou dost share Thyself with Thy creature.

Come, refresh me abundantly with Thyself. For how shall a spark live outside its fire? Or how can a drop of water endure outside its fountain?

Come, let Thy sweet blaze devour and envelop me utterly, spirit and soul, as Thy omnipotent liberality may do with a tiny grain of dust. O Love, O most pleasant noontide Heat, a holy repose in the plenitude of Thy peace is my surpassing delight! Thy longed-for sabbaths are filled with the presence of God and pour forth upon Thy bride the grace of Thy most serene countenance.

[13] Cf. Cant. 1:1.

Come, O my Beloved, chosen and preferred above all creatures, now give me knowledge in Thee and show me where Thou feedest, where Thou liest in the midday.[14] Behold, my spirit burneth with desire of the delightsomeness of Thy repose.

O Love, here under the grateful shadow of Thy charity reposeth all my hope and all my confidence. In the bosom of Thy peace, Israel dwelleth confidently.[15] My soul longeth and ardently yearneth for this solemn sabbath.

O Love, the fruition of Thee is that sacred marriage between the Word and the soul, which is wrought by perfect union with God. To possess Thee, is to be bound up with God. To enjoy Thee, is to be made one with God. Thou art that peace which surpasseth all understanding;[16] Thou art the path whereby the bridechamber is attained.

Oh had I but the happiness, despite my wretchedness, to repose for a moment under the blessed shadow of Thy love, that my heart might be strengthened! Had I but one consoling utterance of Thy living Word, that my soul might hear from Thy mouth these good and welcome tidings: "I am thy salvation;[17] behold, the sanctuary of My Heart now openeth wide unto thee!"

And why, O Love most exalted, shouldst Thou have loved anyone so ill-favored and so base, unless it were to give her beauty in Thee? Thy tender charity winneth and draweth me, O Thou exquisite Flower sprung of the Virgin Mary!

In my expectation let me not be put to shame,[18] but grant me to find rest for my soul in Thee. Nothing have I found more desirable, nothing have I counted more lovable, nothing dearer have I desired, than to be infolded, O Love, in Thy embrace, to rest beneath the wings of my Jesus, and to dwell in the tabernacles of Divine charity.

O Love, O beautiful Noonday, it is my desire to die a thou-

---

[14] *Ibid.* 1:6. [15] Cf. Jer. 23:6. [16] Phil. 4:7.
[17] Ps. 34:3. [18] Cf. Ps. 118:116.

sand times, that my rest may be in Thee. Oh that Thou, dear as Thou art, wouldst incline Thy face towards me, in all the goodness and beauty of Thy fair love!

Oh that it were given me to draw exceeding close unto Thee, that I might find myself not merely nigh Thee but even within Thee; that by Thee, the Sun of Justice, the flowers of all the virtues might spring up in me, who am now but dust and ashes; and that my soul, wedded unto Thee, might be blessed with such fecundity that the glorious fruit of all perfection might ripen in me! Then freed from this vale of misery and beholding Thy face, which is the object of my desires, I should glory eternally because Thou, O unspotted Mirror, hadst not disdained to be united in verity with a soul so sinful as mine!

O CHARITY, at the hour of my death, let thy words, which are better than wine,[19] refresh me, and let thy lips, which are sweeter than honey and the honeycomb,[20] console me; and be thou thyself my way, lest in that hour I should go astray in crooked paths. Thou wilt help me, O queen, to attain unhindered unto the lovely and fruitful lands of the Divine wilderness; there may I deserve to enjoy in never-ending happiness the glorious presence of my Bridegroom, yea, of Him who is God, of Him who is the Lamb. And let all things say: Amen.

3

In the evening thou shalt long and faint with anticipation of enjoying the eternal vision of the glorious face of God and of the Lamb; and thou shalt cast thyself into the embrace of Jesus, thy Bridegroom and thy Lover, like a busy bee, clinging with thy soul's kiss unto His loving Heart. Thou shalt ask of him the heavenly kiss that will make thee die unto thyself, that by this death thou mayest pass over into God and become one spirit with Him.[21] In thy thirst

---

[19] Cf. Cant. 1:1.   [20] Ps. 18:11; cf. Cant. 4:11.   [21] Cf. 1 Cor. 6:17.

for God, cry out unto Him in the words of these verses from Psalm 41:

As the hart panteth after the fountains of water, so my soul panteth after Thee, O God.

My soul hath thirsted after the strong living God; when shall I come and appear before the face of God?

My tears have been my bread day and night, whilst it is said unto me daily: "Where is thy God?"

Then add the following prayer:

Come, O Love, with Thy all-heavenly kiss, Thou art the fountain for which I thirst. Behold, my heart burneth for Thee; how great is my desire that Thou, O Sea of immensity, shouldst absorb me like a tiny drop of water in Thee! Thou art for my soul a Portal, living and most lovely, through which I may enter into Thee and bid farewell to myself.

Come, open unto me the portal of salvation of Thy most beloved Heart. Behold, I no longer have my own heart with me, but Thou, O my dearest Treasure, dost keep it with Thee in Thy closed chamber. Thou art all my wealth, most dearly cherished by my heart. Unto Thee alone my soul doth cleave with all its ardor.

Oh, how ineffable is union with Thee! In truth, intimacy with Thee is far more precious than life itself. From Thee exhaleth the penetrating fragrance of the balsam of peace and of merciful forgiveness. Thou art the treasury that superaboundeth with Divine consolations. O CHARITY, queen that thou art, bring me into thy storerooms,[22] that I may taste the sweetness of the best wines which are hidden there! Behold, all thy vessels are filled unto the brim with God and overflowing with the Holy Spirit.

Oh if I but had my desire, and if my choice were but granted

---

[22] Cf. Cant. 1:3.

me, that in very truth Thou shouldst turn Thee towards me and shouldst refresh me with the exquisite kiss of Thy merciful forgiveness! O my most dearly Beloved, would that in my inmost being I might take hold of Thee and kiss Thee, to be united with Thee in verity, to cleave unto Thee, and nevermore to be parted from Thee!

O Love, O Holy Spirit, Thou art the all-sweet Kiss of the holy Trinity, which doth so powerfully unite the Father and the Son. Thou art that Kiss of salvation which the ever-reigning Godhead hath impressed upon our humanity through the Son.

O heavenly Kiss, let me not slip from Thy bonds in my littleness and lowliness; lavish upon me Thy touch and Thy embrace, until I become one spirit with God.[23] Let it be mine to experience in verity how great is the delight of embracing Thee in Thyself and of being united unto Thee, the living God, my most cherished Love.

O Love, O God, Thou art my dearest possession, and apart from Thee I neither hope, nor wish for, nor desire aught else in heaven or on earth. Thou art my true inheritance and all my expectation; Thou art my sole aim, and all my intent is to gain Thee.

Come, O Love, let Thy perfect love for me be my end and my perfection. When evening falleth, show me the covenant of spiritual marriage which my heart now entereth upon with Thee. In the countenance of my God, whom I love surpassingly, Thou art the Light of the evening star. O my beloved and glorious Evening, graciously appear unto me at the hour of my death, that I may have in Thee the long-desired evening of my sojourn upon earth, and gently fall asleep and take my repose in the blessed haven of Thy breast.

O Love, O God, Thou who art my deliverance, graciously infold my soul within Thee; then, arrayed in Thee and in Thy regal beauty, I shall appear worthily in the presence of my

23 Cf. 1 Cor. 6:17.

eternal Bridegroom, clad in my wedding garment and bearing my bridal dowry.

Come, O Love, let the hour of my life's ending be stamped with the seal of Thy dear affection and imprinted with the mark of Thy unending forgiveness, that Thy blessing may rain down upon me in its fulness and bring me without hindrance unto the portal of my eternal reception into Thee, to the portal of everlasting fruition and endless possession.

O Love, O my dearly beloved Evening, in the hour of my death may I behold Thee gladly and joyfully! May that holy flame which, in the fiery omnipotence of the Godhead, burneth in Thee eternally, purge out every stain from my soul most verily.

O my all-sweet Evening, when the evening of this life closeth in about me, grant that I may be sweetly lulled to sleep in Thee and experience that most blessed rest which is prepared in Thee for Thy beloved! May Thy fair love look upon me with all its calm and loveliness, and deign to set in order and dispose the splendid preparations for my nuptials. By the riches of Thy bounty, cover over my poverty and conceal the neediness of my ignoble life. In the delights of Thy charity, let my soul dwell with exceeding trust.

Then, O Love, be Thou Thyself my Evening, that in Thee my soul, with joy and exultation, may bid my body a fond farewell, and in Thy shade my spirit, returning unto the Lord who gave it, may softly rest in peace. Then shalt Thou say unto me clearly, Thy voice resounding like a melodious harp: "Behold, the Bridegroom is at hand! [24] Go forth now and draw yet nearer unto Him, that the glory of His countenance may make thee glad!"

Oh how happy, how blessed, is the man whose earthly sojourning endeth in Thee! Woe is me! How long shall my sojourning be prolonged? Oh what will this *Then* be like, when

[24] Cf. Matt. 25:6.

[93]

there shall come for me that sweet and most delightful *Now,* wherein the glory of my God, my King, and my Bridegroom shall be revealed and shall appear unto me, with never-ending joy in Him and everlasting happiness? When in all truth I shall contemplate and behold that lovely face of my Jesus, which I have sought and desired, and for whose beauty my soul hath thirsted and yearned so long? Then most certainly shall I be satisfied and made full by the torrent of His pleasure, which now hath been so long concealed from me in the treasure house of the Godhead. Then shall I behold and contemplate my God, my dearest Love, for whom now my spirit and my heart have fainted away.[25]

Oh when wilt Thou show me Thyself, that I may behold Thee and may draw waters with delight from Thee, O God, who art the living Fountain? Then shall I drink and be inebriated with the plenitude of the sweetness of the living Fountain, which poureth forth from the delights of the glorious face of Him whom my soul desireth.

O lovely Face, when wilt Thou satisfy me with Thyself? Then shall I go into the place of the wonderful tabernacle, even into the sight of God, before the portal of whose presence chamber my heart groaneth because of the length of my sojourning. Oh when wilt Thou fill me with happiness by Thy glorious face? Then shall I contemplate, then shall I kiss my Jesus, the true Bridegroom of my soul, to whom my whole being already cleaveth in its dryness, and towards whom it reacheth out with its every fibre.

Oh, who will deliver me from the exile of this pilgrimage? Oh, who will release me from the snares of this world? Oh, when shall I leave this wretched body behind, that I may behold Thee without a veil, O Love, O God, O Star of stars? In Thee, O dearest Love, I shall be released from the temptations of this mortal life; in Thee, O God my Lover, I shall leap over the

[25] Cf. Ps. 72:26.

[94]

wall [26] of the body and find myself in that place of security and of rejoicing where I shall behold Thee no longer in a dark manner but in truth and face to face.

Come, Thou Fountain of everlasting light, draw me back unto Thyself, unto the abyss of the ocean of Thy Being (whence I issued forth by Thy creative act), where I may know as I am known [27] and love as I am loved; that I may see Thee, my God, as Thou art, [28] and be blessed for evermore in the vision, fruition, and possession of Thyself. Amen.

II

On this same day of love, thou shalt offer thy soul unto the Lord seven times, that He may refresh within thee thy love for His Divine Heart.

1

And first at the hour of Matins pray unto the Lord, the most perfect of all masters, that by the anointing of His Spirit He may teach thee the art of love, accepting thee as His own disciple, that under His tutorship thou mayest be exercised unremittingly in the virtue of charity. Thou shalt recite this verse and prayer:

VERSE. O Lord, Jesus Christ, to Thee have I fled. Teach me to do Thy will, for Thou art my God. [29]

PRAYER

O Love, O Master, O my Lord, Thou who art higher than the heavens and deeper than the abyss, the vision of whose marvelous wisdom is the beatitude of all Thy creatures! Thou whose charity hath no limits, who art above the cherubim, [30]

---

26 Cf. Ps. 17:30.   27 Cf. 1 Cor. 13:12.   28 Cf. 1 John 3:2.
29 Ps. 142:10.   30 Cf. Isai. 37:16.

dost look down upon the lowly [31] in this vale of tears and dost gather the little children to instruct them in the ways of salvation; come, refuse not Thy lessons unto me in my meanness, but refresh me, I beseech Thee, with Thy lifegiving doctrine. Adopt me as Thy daughter, that Thou mayest possess me as all Thy own, for this is the desire of my heart! Come, O Love, begin at once to teach me; separate me from myself for the ministry of Thy living charity and affection, and, O Love, possess, sanctify, and utterly fill my spirit. Amen.

2

At the hour of Prime pray unto the Lord, that He may admit thee into the school of love, where thou mayest learn yet more fully how to know and to love Jesus. Now therefore recite this verse and prayer:

VERSE. I am Thy handmaid, O Jesus most loving! Give me understanding, that I may learn Thy commandments. [32]

PRAYER

O Love, O God, with what great care Thou dost warm Thy little ones and give them nourishment in the bosom of Thy charity, even as the hen tendeth her chickens! Open straightway unto me the school of chaste love, for this is the desire of my heart! There let me hear Thy precious teachings, and through Thee let my soul attain unto goodness, [33] nay even unto holiness and perfection in truth.

Come, O Love, immerse my spirit so deeply in Thy charity, that through Thee I may become a child gifted with understanding, and Thou Thyself mayest be in truth my Father, Teacher, and Master. Then by Thy fatherly blessing let my spirit be completely purified and refined from all the dross of sin, that it may be altogether ready and apt to receive Thy burning words, and

[31] Cf. Ps. 112:6.　　　[32] Cf. Ps. 118:73.　　　[33] Cf. Wisd. 8:19.

Thy Holy Spirit, O Love, Thy right and perfect Spirit, may dwell within my whole being. Amen.

3

At the hour of Terce pray unto the Lord, that He may write the burning law of His Divine love in thy heart with the living letters of His Spirit, that thou mayest ever and always cleave closely unto Him. Now therefore recite this verse and prayer:

VERSE. Oh that all my thoughts, words, and works may be directed to keep Thy justifications,[34] most loving Jesus, at all times!

PRAYER

O Love, O God, how present Thou art unto them that seek Thee! How kind, how lovable unto them that find Thee! Oh if Thou wouldst but explain unto me now Thy wondrous Alphabet, that my heart may have one lesson therein from Thee! Teach me to know by living experience the essence of the glorious *Alpha* which is the beginning of Thy fair love, and hide not from me that *Beta* which doth produce the rich and abundant fruits of Thy ever-reigning wisdom. With the finger of God, which is Thy Spirit,[35] point out unto me carefully, one by one, each letter of Thy charity, that I may in truth examine, consider, learn, know, and recognize them (so far as is lawful in this life) with the pure eyes of my heart, until I attain a foretaste of Thy delights.

Teach me by the cooperation of Thy Spirit the *Tau* of supreme perfection, and guide me unto the *Omega* of complete consummation. Grant that in this life I may so perfectly learn Thy scripture, full of charity and love, that to fill up Thy charity in me, not one *Iota* may be wanting, lest thereby I might be

34 Cf. Ps. 118:5.   35 See Luke 11:20.

made to tarry when Thou, O Love, O God, O my kindest Love, callest me unto Thee, to contemplate Thee Thyself, in Thyself, eternally. Amen.

4

At the hour of Sext pray unto the Lord that thou mayest make such progress in the art of loving Him, that His love may use thee as its own instrument according to all His will, and thou mayest be fashioned entirely after God's Heart. Now therefore recite this verse and prayer:

VERSE. O my beloved Jesus, Thou true Lawgiver, give me Thy dearest blessing, that I may go on from strength unto strength and behold Thee, the God of gods, in Sion.[36]

PRAYER

O Love, O God, whoever loveth Thee not is a babe incapable of speech; and none shall grow unto maturity save him who cleaveth with his whole being unto Thee and constantly offereth unto Thee all his love. Come, let not me alone be thus ever left behind in Thy school of charity, like a tiny chick that hath not yet been hatched to profit by Thy care; but in Thee and through Thee, or rather with Thee, let me grow into maturity day by day and advance from strength unto strength, daily bringing forth fruit unto Thee, my Beloved, in the new path of Thy love. Nor doth it suffice me to know Thee only by the syllables of Thy name; I wish, I long, and I greatly desire to know Thee with understanding, to love Thee mightily, to fix my affections upon Thee with ravishment, yea, but also with wisdom, and to cleave unto Thee deathlessly, that I may now begin to live no longer in myself but in Thee alone. Now, O Love, make Thyself known unto me in truth and enthrone Thyself in my soul in all holiness. Amen.

[36] Cf. Ps. 83:8.

5

At the hour of None pray unto the Lord that He, the King of Kings, may enroll thee in the service of love and teach thee to take the sweet yoke and light burden upon thee, that thou mayest follow thy Lord with thy cross and cleave unto thy God with deathless love. Now therefore recite this verse and prayer:

VERSE. Thou, O Lord, art my hope, my protector, and my refuge; Thou art with me in all my tribulation.[37]

PRAYER

O Love, O God, if anyone proveth himself both quick and steadfast in the work of Thy love, he shall stand for ever in the presence of Thy majesty. Come, O CHARITY, thou queen of queens, for thy glory let me ally myself with thee in the new service of thy affection. Teach me to put out my hand to works of strength [38] and in Thee and through Thee to undertake and perform, quickly and unwearyingly, the offices of Thy love. Gird my thigh with the sword of Thy Spirit, O Thou most mighty,[39] and give me a manly heart, that I may strive after the virtues manfully and resolutely, and, in firm reliance upon Thee, persevere at Thy side invincibly.

Let me devote all my forces so fully to the demands of Thy charity and so far fix and establish my thoughts in Thee, that despite the weakness of my sex, I may attain, by strength of soul and virility of mind, to that manner of love which bringeth one unto the secret apartment of the nuptial chamber of perfect union with Thee. Now, O Love, hold and possess me as Thy own, for henceforth I have neither spirit nor soul save in Thee. Amen.

6

At the hour of Vespers, with Jesus thy Lover, go forward

[37] Cf. Ps. 90:2, 15.   [38] Cf. Prov. 31:19.   [39] Cf. Eph. 6:17; Ps. 44:4.

in safety to meet every temptation with the armor of thy Lover, that in Him (whose mercy ever helpeth and comforteth thee) thou mayest be able to overcome thy own flesh, the world, and the devil, and to triumph gloriously over every temptation. Ask for such victory by this verse and prayer:

VERSE. O my kindest Jesus, suffer not my foot to be moved; for behold, Thou dost neither slumber nor sleep, Thou who keepest my soul.[40]

PRAYER

O Love, O God, Thou Thyself art my wall and my bulwark.[41] Behold, they who endure anguish in this world know what a shade is spread above them in Thy peace, as a protection from the heat and from the rain.[42] Come, look now upon me and see the battle which I sustain, and do Thou Thyself teach my fingers to war.[43] If armies in camp should stand together against me, my heart shall not fear,[44] for Thou Thyself, O my faithful rampart, my strong tower, art with me both within and without.

If Thou dost help me, where is my adversary? If Thou art for me, let him advance against me! Thou dost show me the plots of Satan at a glance, and with a word, as if with the merest puff, Thou dost blow them out of my path. If my enemy throweth me down a thousand times, will not Thy dearest right hand reach out unto me as I fall? I shall embrace this hand of Thine and kiss it lovingly; with Thee to fight for me and defend me, I shall stand firm against every danger and suffer no harm.

Do Thou within me tread Satan underfoot[45] and bring to naught and utterly discomfit all my faults. In Thy presence let a thousand fall at my side and ten thousand at my right hand.[46]

---

40 Cf. Ps. 120:3-4.   41 Cf. Isai. 26:1.   42 See *ibid.* 4:6.
43 Cf. Ps. 143:1.   44 Ps. 26:3.   45 Cf. Rom. 16:20.
46 Cf. Ps. 90:7.

But evil shall not approach me, since Thou Thyself art with me, O my sublime Truth and dearest Good! Oh that at last Thou wouldst turn Thy sharp arrows[47] against me! Oh that Thou wouldst pierce my heart with the lance of Thy love, that I may dwell with all the more confidence in the midst of Thee,[48] O Charity, and in Thee! Now, O Love, let me so fall here beneath Thy assault, that I may not slip from between Thy hands for all eternity. Amen.

7

At the hour of Compline, present unto the Lord thy eager desires: to be inebriated with the wine of love poured out for thee by thy Beloved; to forget the world in union with God; to pass over from thyself into the embrace of thy Beloved; and, putting off the last remnants of thy human weakness, gently to fall asleep upon the breast of Jesus. Thus thou shalt daily die unto thyself in love and live unto God alone, and in death's hour thou shalt with confidence meet death, looking upon it as the end of thy exile, the door of the kingdom, and the gate of heaven. Now therefore recite this verse and prayer:

VERSE. Hide me, O most loving Jesus, in the secret of Thy face,[49] from all who lie in wait for me; and let not my soul be put to shame when she shall speak to her enemies in the gate,[50] but fill her with happiness by Thy glorious face.

PRAYER

O Love, O God, Thou art the consummation and end of all good; all whom Thou hast chosen, Thou lovest unto the end; whatsoever cometh into Thy hands Thou wilt not cast out,[51] but wilt keep for Thyself with exceeding care. Come, appropriate unto Thyself both my whole being and the end of my

---

[47] Ps. 44:6.　　　　[48] Cf. Jer. 23:6.　　　　[49] Cf. Ps. 30:21.
[50] Cf. Ps. 126:5.　　　[51] Cf. John 6:37.

perfection, by right of everlasting possession. From this moment spare me no longer, but wound the depths of my heart until my very spirit is transpierced, that Thou mayest leave within me not one spark of life. Nay rather, transport my whole life with Thee, keeping back my soul in Thee for Thyself.

Who will grant me, O Charity, to be perfected in Thee, to be freed from the prison of this body through death bestowed by Thee, and to be delivered from this sojourning? What a blessing, O Love, to behold Thee, to enjoy Thee, and to possess Thee for eternity! On the day of my death do Thou comfort me richly by Thy presence, and bless me then in the fair dawn of the contemplation of Thee face to face. Now, O Love, I here bequeath and commend unto Thee my life and my soul both together; suffer me now in peace to rest and to sleep [52] in Thee. Amen.

III

In the course of this day which thou hast given over unto love, devote thyself unto earnest meditation, that thy heart may take fire from the true Sun which is God, and this fire may never go out within thee, but thou mayest grow in love from day unto day. To this end choose one of these verses:

Blessed are the eyes that see Thee, O Love, O God! Oh when shall I come thither where Thou, O God, art the true Light, God and the Lamb? I know that at last I shall behold Thee with my eyes, O Jesus, my God and my Saviour!

Blessed are the ears that hear Thee, O Love, O God, O Word of life! Oh when shall I hear the unearthly music of Thy voice, comforting me and calling me unto Thee? Come, let me not fear the hearing of condemnation,[53] but let me speedily hear Thy voice calling me unto glory. Amen.

Blessed are the nostrils that breathe Thee in, O Love, O God,

[52] Cf. Ps. 4:9.　　　[53] Cf. Ps. 111:7.

Thou fragrance of life! Oh when will the heavenly scent of Thy Divinity breathe round about me? Pray let me come speedily unto the fertile and delightful pastures of the eternal vision of Thee. Amen.

Blessed is the mouth that tasteth, O Love, O God, Thy words of consolation, sweeter than honey and the honeycomb! Oh when will my soul be filled with the riches of Thy Godhead [54] and inebriated with the plenitude of Thy delights? Come, Lord, here on earth let me so taste that Thou art sweet, [55] that there in heaven I may have the happiness of enjoying Thee, O God of my life, for all eternity. Amen.

Blessed is the soul that cleaveth unto Thee in the embrace of deathless love, and blessed is the heart that doth experience the kiss of Thy Heart, O Love, O God, entering upon an inviolable nuptial bond with Thee! Oh when shall I be held in the arms of Thy blessedness and come to behold Thee, O God of my heart, without a veil? Come, snatch me speedily from this exile, and let me with jubilation behold Thy glorious face! Amen.

Finally, to obtain confirmation in love, abandon and resign thyself entirely unto the control of love, cleaving with thy whole being unto God thy Lover, that He may use thee as an instrument wherewith to delight His Divine Heart as He will, and keep thee in Him and Himself in thee, for Himself, unto eternal life. Now therefore recite this prayer:

I hold Thee by my love, O most loving Jesus, and I will not let Thee go, [56] for Thy blessing is in nowise enough for me unless I may hold Thee and possess Thee as my best part, all my hope, and all my expectation. Now, O Love, Thou Life who dost give life, give me life in that living Word of God who is Thyself; thus for whatever part of the love of God has been

[54] Cf. Ps. 62:6.   [55] Cf. Ps. 33:9.   [56] See Gen. 32:26.

wasted and lost within me, do Thou make amends through Thyself.

O Love, O God, who hast created me, in Thy love recreate me. O Love who hast redeemed me, fill up and redeem for Thyself in me whatever part of Thy love hath fallen into neglect within me. O Love, O God, who, to make me Thine, in the blood of Thy Christ hast purchased me, in Thy truth sanctify me.[57] O Love, O God, who hast adopted me as a daughter, after Thy own Heart fashion and foster me. O Love, who as Thine and not another's hast chosen me, grant that I may cleave unto Thee with my whole being. O Love, O God, who hast first loved me, grant that with my whole heart, and with my whole soul, and with my whole strength, I may love Thee.

O Love, O God almighty, in Thy love confirm me. O Love most wise, give me wisdom in the love of Thee. O Love most sweet, give me sweetness in the taste of Thee. O Love most dear, grant that I may live unto Thee alone. O Love most faithful, in all my tribulations comfort and succor me. O Love who art ever with me, work all my works in me.[58] O Love most victorious, grant that I may persevere unto the end in Thee.

O Love most cherished, who hast never forsaken me, unto Thee I commend my spirit. In the hour of my death receive me unto Thyself, calling me unto Thee with Thy own voice and saying: "This day thou shalt be with Me; come forth now from thy exile unto the solemn *Morrow* of that eternity which shall never fade! There thou shalt find Me, Jesus, the true *Today* of the Divine glory, who am the beginning and the end of every created being. In this immutability never again shalt thou know a *Morrow*; but in Me, the true *Today,* thou shalt have an eternal *Today,* that as I live, Thou also shalt live in Me, Jesus, thy God and thy Lover, in the transports of happiness without end!" Let all the powers, all the thoughts, and all the affections of my body and soul say: "Amen!"

[57] Cf. John 17:17.   [58] See Isai. 26:12.

6th Exercise

PRAISE AND THANKSGIVING

Commentary

WHEN anyone has advanced in the love of God far enough to seek, like Saint Gertrude, to live rather in Him than in self, such a person is irresistibly drawn to that praise of God which is the occupation of the blessed who already see Him face to face. A recent writer on the subject of the *Exercises* brings out this yearning of the creature's love to respond to the love of God for man:

> The sixth Exercise on "Praise and Thanksgiving" gives the soul a foretaste of the joys of heaven. Saint Gertrude here reaches the state of prayer which causes the soul to bow down in admiration and wonder at the greatness of God's love. Overwhelmed with awe and gratitude, she sings in their entirety the psalms beginning *Benedic anima mea Domino* and *Exaltabo te, Deus meus Rex,* and [the canticle] *Benedicite.* Each of these psalms is followed by litanies of love which transport the soul beyond the confines of this world. The Exercise ends with the urgent petition that God may continue His love and confirm it in the Beatific Vision.[1]

It will be easier for us to follow Gertrude in her ascent if we study this chapter more in detail. In Part I (the introduction) the soul humbly acknowledges its unworthiness; then little by little it finds courage, in phrases drawn partly from Isaias, to enter on God's praise. Just in the middle of this introduction occurs a fresh allusion to the wound of love; yet another will be found in the first paragraph of the conclusion of the Exercise (Part V).

The body of this Exercise falls into three main divisions (Parts II, III, and IV respectively) unequal in length, but parallel in construction. Each of these parts begins with one of the selections from the Psalter mentioned above. Then follow four groups of prayers; first, a free commentary on the psalm or canticle just recited; second, prayers of praise, throughout which, in Gertrude's original Latin, every sentence begins with either *Benedicant* or *Benedicat* (a word pattern which cannot be reproduced in English with the same effect); third, prayers of jubilation, in which every sentence begins with either *Jubilent* or *Jubilet*; and fourth, prayers of adoration, where Gertrude resumes a less formal composition.

Among the prayers of adoration it should be noticed that those of Part IV are inspired by the thoughts of Psalm 22. In connection with the pasture mentioned in this psalm, Gertrude introduces Saint Bernard's comment, that the gift of contemplation is granted "all too seldom and for too short a time," which appears also in the *Herald.*[2] A few lines further on, she alludes to the sixtieth chapter of Isaias, and then she comes back to the shepherd psalm. She loved to regard Christ as the Shepherd and herself as His ewe lamb; this scriptural figure recurs in other parts of the *Exercises.*[3]

In Part V, she recommends the hour of her death to the protection of Christ and His Mother, and voices her nostalgic longing for heaven in poignant phrases which sustain the beauty of the chapter to the very end.

6th Exercise

PRAISE AND THANKSGIVING

From time to time choose thee a day when thou canst freely give thyself over unto the praise of God, in atonement for all thy failures, during the course of thy life, to offer unto God praise and thanksgiving for all His benefits. This shall be then a day of praise and thanksgiving and a day of jubilee, and thou shalt solemnize it in anticipation of that resplendent praise which will be thy joyful paean unto the Lord in eternity, when thou shalt be satisfied by the presence of God, and thy soul shall be filled with the glory of the Lord. Therefore in this exercise, these heavenly strains are mingled with the devout sighs of the soul who seeketh to behold the face of God.

I

First, then, in the spirit of humility, thou shalt come before the face of thy God, that He may show thee the favor of His countenance; and thou shalt frame thy prayer in this manner:

I will speak unto my Lord, whereas I am dust and ashes.[1] O my God, most high and most exalted, who dost look down upon

[1] Gen. 18:27.

the lowly in the depths of earth, my soul and my spirit faint away at the thought of Thy infinite benefits. Reveal unto me the treasure of Thy most loving Heart, wherein is laid up for me all that I most desire. Reveal unto me the beauty of Thy glorious countenance, that I may pour out my soul in Thy presence.[2] Reveal unto me the wellspring of Thy merciful kindness, which will bring me peace to gladden my soul and to loose my tongue for Thy praise.

Come, o LOVE, do thou enter the presence of the great God in my behalf and utter there the cry of my desire, for already all my strength is withered by reason of my thirst for God. Come, draw my spirit aloft and lift it up unto thee, for already my flesh and my heart have fainted away at the thought of God my Saviour.[3] Come, present me unto my Lord the King, for already my soul melteth[4] with love while I await my Bridegroom. Now, o LOVE, satisfy my desire most speedily; if thou wilt tarry, I shall be found already at the point of death, fainting away for love.

Here thou shalt take up the Lord's praises:

Arise, O my soul, shake thyself from the dust, rise up,[5] and enter into the presence of the Lord thy God, to confess before Him all His mercies and the great tenderness which He hath shown thee. And what shall I say unto the Lord, or how can I make any answer when He speaketh?[6] o LOVE, I suffer violence; answer thou for me,[7] because I know not what to say unto the God of my life. I am become speechless with wonder at the glory of His countenance, and I am bereft now of voice and of thought alike, for my heart and my strength have fainted away at the splendor of His majesty. o LOVE, in Jesus, my God, the Word of life, do thou answer for me and move in my favor

2 Cf. Ps. 141:3.   3 Ps. 72:26.   4 Cf. Cant. 5:6.
5 See Isai. 51:17, 52:1-2.   6 Cf. Job 9:3.   7 Isai. 38:14.

His divine Heart, wherein all thy power shineth forth so brilliantly.

O LOVE, my strength returneth, and through thee I will say unto the God of my salvation: "Thou art the Helper of my soul! [8] Thou art the life of my spirit! Thou art the God of my heart!" [9]

O LOVE, do thou take in hand most reverently that all-glorious lyre of the throat of Jesus my Bridegroom, that He Himself, the God of my life, may sound the first word of praise unto Himself on my behalf and thus infold both my life and my soul in the delight of His praise. Now come, O LOVE, that which thou dost, do quickly. For I can no longer endure the fierce wound wherewith thou hast pierced me.

Here thou shalt stir up thy soul to delight in God:

Now, O my soul, lift up thy eyes, behold and look upon the power of thy King, the grace of thy God, the charity of thy Saviour, whom thou hast approached. Be still now, taste and see [10] how sweet and how admirable is that Bridegroom whom, out of thousands, thou hast chosen.[11] See what is that glory, defying all comparison with the world, which, for its sake, thou hast despised. See what is that supreme Good which thou hast awaited. See what is that country after which thou hast sighed. See what is that crown for which thou hast labored. See what is that essence, what that infinite greatness of thy God, whom thou hast loved, whom thou hast adored, whom thou hast always desired.

O God of my life, I know not how to praise Thee worthily; I know not what to give back unto Thee, my Beloved, for all the blessings which Thou hast given unto me.[12] Therefore, my dearest Jesus, I offer Thee as a holocaust of praise, Thyself in

8 Cf. Ps. 53:6. 9 Ps. 72:26. 10 Cf. Ps. 45:11; Ps. 33:9.
11 Cf. Cant. 5:10. 12 Cf. Ps. 115:12.

me, and myself in Thee; naught more do I possess; my being and my life in Thee, all this do I give Thee.

Thou art my life. Thou art my sufficiency. Thou art my glory. Thou art the revelation of that mercy which is displayed so wondrously in my soul. Unto Thee be the highest praise and thanksgiving. Oh when shall I offer my inmost soul amid the flames upon Thy altar? When shall I set my heart ablaze with that sacred fire (which ever burneth there), and immolate my entire self unto Thee as a sacrifice of praise?

O my God, Thy holiness is my delight! Come, enlarge my heart in Thee and make wide my soul, that my whole being may be filled with Thy glory. Oh when will these words be spoken unto my soul: "Turn thee into thy rest, for the Lord hath been bountiful unto thee"?[13] Oh when shall I hear that welcome cry: "Come, enter thou into the nuptial chamber of thy Bridegroom"? O Jesus, Thou who art my peace ineffable, when shall I rest and fall asleep in Thee, that I may see Thy glory?

But Thou, O Life of my spirit, hast the power to keep what I have entrusted unto Thee and to bring back my soul unto Thyself, who hast created me. O LOVE, when wilt thou lead my soul forth from its prison? Oh when wilt thou free it from the fetters of the body? When, oh when wilt thou bring me into the marriage chamber of my Bridegroom, that I may be united unto Him in deathless joy? Come, O Love, hasten my nuptials, for I would gladly die a thousand deaths in order to experience such delights; yet what I seek is not my own advantage but Thy good pleasure.

II

Then as if thou wert fainting away with wonder at the glory of thy God, stand before the countenance of Him upon

[13] Ps. 114:7.

whom the angels have desired to look, and recite with thy heart and with thy lips the first of the psalms beginning: "Bless the Lord":

PSALM 102

Bless the Lord, O my soul, and all that is within me bless His holy name.

Bless the Lord, O my soul, and never forget all He hath done for thee;

Who forgiveth all thy iniquities; who healeth all thy diseases;

Who redeemeth thy life from destruction; who crowneth thee with mercy and compassion;

Who satisfieth thy desire with good things; thy youth shall be renewed like the eagle's.

The Lord doth mercies and judgment for all that suffer wrong.

He hath made His ways known unto Moses, His will unto the children of Israel.

The Lord is compassionate and merciful, longsuffering and plenteous in mercy.

He will not always be angry, nor will He threaten for ever.

He hath not dealt with us according to our sins nor rewarded us according to our iniquities.

For according to the height of the heaven above the earth, He hath strengthened His mercy towards them that fear Him.

As far as the east is from the west, so far hath He removed our iniquities from us.

As a father hath compassion upon his children, so hath the Lord compassion upon them that fear Him;

For He knoweth our frame; He remembereth that we are dust.

Man's days are as grass; as the flower of the field so shall he flourish.

For the spirit shall pass in him, and he shall not be; and he shall know his place no more.

But the mercy of the Lord is from eternity and unto eternity, upon them that fear Him;

And His justice unto children's children, unto such as keep His covenant and are mindful of His commandments to do them.

The Lord hath prepared His throne in heaven, and His kingdom shall rule over all.

Bless the Lord, all ye His angels, you that are mighty in strength and execute His word, hearkening unto the voice of His orders.

Bless the Lord, all ye His hosts, you ministers of His that do His will.

Bless the Lord, all His works, in every place of His dominion; O my soul, bless thou the Lord.

1

Now pay homage unto the glorious face of thy God with these words:

Blessed art Thou, O Adonai, in the firmament of heaven. Let my spirit bless Thee with its inmost being and all its strength. Let the whole substance of my soul and body bless Thee. Let everything within me glorify Thee. Let all my desires cry out unto Thee together, because Thou alone deservest praise and glory for evermore. Now my heart and my strength desert me, and the inmost being of my spirit doth slip away after Thee, O God my Lover, who didst create me for Thyself; and my soul which Thou hast redeemed, lamenting that my sojourning upon earth is not yet ended, followeth Thee in spirit into the sanctuary where Thou Thyself, O my King and my God, dost abide with the substance of my human flesh.

Oh how blessed are they who dwell in Thy house! [14] And

[14] Ps. 83:5.

how incomparably more blessed are they who behold Thee face to face in Thy majesty! They in truth shall praise Thee for evermore because of Thy immense glory. Oh when shall my soul gain admission into the courts of Thy wondrous tabernacle,[15] where my lips shall praise Thee with all these saints of Thine, joyfully crying out: "Holy, Holy, Holy!" in the presence of Thy majesty for evermore?

O my God, how glorious Thou art upon the holy throne of Thy Godhead! Thou deservest all love and all praise. Thy splendor is the delight of my eyes; what happiness it is to behold Thee who art the true Sun! How lovely, harmonious, and beautiful is the praise that is paid unto Thee, where thousands of thousands of angels stand before Thee! My heart and soul already fly thither in their eagerness, leaving me behind, that they may exult in Thee, the living God. O Thou whose holiness is my delight, how infinite is Thy glory before the holy throne of Thy majesty, where all Thy angels and saints praise Thee!

Behold, my soul already groweth weary and faint because of the irksomeness of this life, and with all my heart I desire the dissolution of my earthly ties, that I may be with Thee. Then, although I am the least [16] of all Thy creatures, I too shall offer Thee rich holocausts of jubilation in company with the blessed who in heaven proclaim Thy praise. There upon the golden altar of Thy Divine Heart, I will burn before Thee the precious incense of my spirit and my soul, with the richness of Thy own sweetness wherewith Thou, O my Father and my Lord, hast so often anointed and consoled me in all my trials and distress.

2

Now break forth into a cry of praise:

O God of my life, let all Thy wondrous works and all the bountiful gifts which I hold from Thee, bless, glorify, and mag-

---

[15] Cf. Ps. 41:5. [16] 1 Cor. 4:13.

nify Thee on my behalf! O God of my heart, let Thy great tenderness and Thy many mercies bless Thee, together with the infinite favors whereby Thou hast done good unto my soul. Let everything within me and all my substance and my strength bless Thee, for Thou art the God of my salvation and the protector of my soul.

3

Now sing jubilantly unto the Lord before the throne of God and of the Lamb,[17] because of all the favors He hath bestowed:

Let the desires and prayers of my heart sing jubilantly unto Thee, and Thy gifts of so many graces chant Thy praises. Let the groans and sighs of my sad sojourning on this earth sing jubilantly unto Thee, and let my expectation and patience bless Thee as I await my long-deferred hope which is Thyself, O my God. Let my hope and confidence in Thee sing jubilantly unto Thee, because Thou, O my God, who art the Life most blessed, wilt one day bring me back unto Thee from the dust.

Let the seal of faith wherewith Thou hast marked me sing jubilantly unto Thee, because I believe that one day these same eyes of mine shall behold Thee, O my dear Redeemer.[18] Let my desire for Thee and the thirst for Thee which I endure sing jubilantly unto Thee, because after this life I shall one day come unto Thee, O my God, who art my true homeland. And let Thy Divine love which, anticipating mine, obligeth me to love Thee without ceasing, most of all sing jubilantly unto Thee, because Thou, O my God, whom I deeply love, art alone God blessed for evermore.

4

Now thou shalt adore before the face of the Lord thy God,

[17] Cf. Apoc. 22:1.   [18] See Job 19:25-26.

*praying devoutly with thy heart and thy lips that Jesus may
fill up the measure of praise which it is beyond thy power
to offer:*

O most loving Jesus, when shall I go into Thy house with
holocausts,[19] that I may offer Thee there a sacrifice of praise [20]
and pay Thee my vows which my lips have uttered when I was
in trouble? [21] When shall I come and show myself before Thy
holy throne, that I may see the glory of Thy countenance, whose
Divine light of itself doth satisfy the desire of all the saints and
set them singing, with hearts and voices, one jubilant song?

Come, O my Beloved, Thou whom I greatly desire, understand my cry. Hearken unto my prayer and graciously hear me,
O my King and my God,[22] for the sighs of my heart and the
desires of my soul do call upon Thee, do yearn for Thee, and
do search after Thee. My eyes shed tears of longing for Thee,
and my gaze seeketh Thee. Thou Thyself art my God, my joy
and my Love, my hope since the days of my youth; [23] Thou
Thyself art all that I wish for, all that I hope for, all that I long
for.

Now, O my Beloved, in my human flesh Thou sittest at the
right hand of the Father in the triumph of Thy love. There Thou
dost keep me for Thyself, written upon Thy hands [24] and Thy
feet and upon Thy most loving Heart, that Thou mayest never
forget my soul which Thou hast redeemed and made Thine at
such great cost. O my God and my mercy, for all the favors
which Thou hast granted, dost grant, and wilt yet grant me, do
Thou now offer unto Thyself on my behalf eternal, infinite, and
immutable praise, for Thou art possessed of all power in Thyself, and Thou knowest what honor befitteth Thy glory and Thy
majesty, unto which all reverence is due. O dearest Jesus, sing
on my behalf a hymn of thanksgiving worthy of Thee, my Lord,

[19] Cf. Ps. 65:13.   [20] Ps. 26:6.   [21] Cf. Ps. 65:13-14.
[22] Cf. Ps. 5:2-3.   [23] Ps. 70:5.   [24] See Isai. 49:16.

who art so mighty and so wonderful. Praise Thyself in Thyself, in me and for me, with all the strength of Thy Godhead, with all the affection of Thy Manhood, on behalf of the whole universe, until Thou dost bring me—the tiniest of all Thy creatures —by Thyself, who art the Way, even unto Thyself, who art the Truth, and dost receive me and hide me in Thyself, who art the Life,[25] that the vision of Thy face with all its glories may be my lot for all eternity.

III

Now as if delighted and refreshed with wonder at the glory of God, thou shalt read the heavenly psalm:

PSALM 144

I will extol Thee, O God my King; and I will bless Thy name for ever, yea, for ever and ever.

Every day will I bless Thee; and I will praise Thy name for ever, yea, for ever and ever.

Great is the Lord and greatly to be praised; and of His greatness there is no end.

Generation and generation shall praise Thy works; and they shall declare Thy power.

They shall speak of the magnificence of the glory of Thy holiness and shall tell Thy wondrous works.

And they shall speak of the might of Thy terrible acts and shall declare Thy greatness.

They shall publish the memory of the abundance of Thy sweetness and shall rejoice in Thy justice.

The Lord is gracious and merciful, patient and plenteous in mercy.

The Lord is sweet unto all, and His tender mercies are over all His works.

25 Cf. John 14:6.

Let all Thy works, O Lord, praise Thee, and let Thy saints bless Thee.

They shall speak of the glory of Thy kingdom and shall tell of Thy power,

To make Thy might known unto the sons of men, and the glory of the magnificence of Thy kingdom.

Thy kingdom is a kingdom of all ages, and Thy dominion endureth throughout all generations.

The Lord is faithful in all His words and holy in all His works.

The Lord lifteth up all that fall and setteth up all that are cast down.

The eyes of all hope in Thee, O Lord, and Thou givest them meat in due season.

Thou openest Thy hand and fillest with blessing every living creature.

The Lord is just in all His ways and holy in all His works.

The Lord is nigh unto all them that call upon Him, unto all that call upon Him in truth.

He will do the will of them that fear Him, and He will hear their prayer and save them.

The Lord keepeth all them that love Him, but all the wicked He will destroy.

My mouth shall speak the praise of the Lord; and let all flesh bless His holy name for ever, yea, for ever and ever.

1

Now pay homage unto God thy Lover with these words:

O my King and my God, Thou who art my Love and my joy, my soul and my heart sing jubilantly unto Thee. My heart desireth to pay Thee homage, to praise Thee, to magnify Thee, and to bless Thee, O Thou Life of my soul, O my God, Thou living and true God, Thou Fountain of eternal light, the light of whose glorious face hath set its mark upon me despite my unworthiness! I offer Thee all the powers of my soul and of my body as a holocaust of ever new praise and of profound thanksgiving.

And what shall I give back unto Thee, my Lord, for all Thy blessings which Thou hast given unto me? [26] For indeed, as I perceive, Thou hast loved me more than Thy own glory, and for my sake Thou hast not spared Thyself. Thou hast created me for Thyself, and hast redeemed me unto Thyself, and hast chosen me, all to the end that Thou mightest bring me unto Thyself, and that Thou mightest grant me the life of beatitude in Thee and eternal felicity in the fruition of Thee. For what have I now in heaven apart from Thee, or which good gift of Thine do I covet or desire apart from Thee?

Thou, O Lord, art my hope, Thou art my glory, Thou art my joy, Thou art my beatitude. Thou art He for whom my spirit thirsteth. Thou art the life of my soul. Thou art the jubilation of my heart. Where shall my wonder lead me, my God, if not unto Thee? Thou art the beginning and the end of all that is good, and all possessors of joy have their common dwelling in Thee. Thou art He who calleth forth the praise of my heart and of my mouth. Thou art all golden in the springtide loveliness of Thy joy-giving love. Let Thy ineffable Godhead magnify and glorify Thee, for Thou art the origin of perpetual light and the Fountain of life. No creature can give Thee the praise that is Thy due. Thou alone, unto whom nothing is ever wanting, art sufficient unto Thyself. The sweetness of Thy face, sweeter than honey and the honeycomb,[27] is the beatitude of the souls of Thy saints.

2

Now bless the Lord God, thy mighty King, for all His loving mercies:

[26] Cf. Ps. 115:12.   [27] Ps. 18:11.

Let Thy glorious and wonderful light bless Thee, my God, on my behalf, and the sovereign beauty of Thy ineffable majesty praise Thee. Let the transcendent splendor of Thy immense glory bless Thee, and the surpassing might of Thy infinite power praise Thee. Let the incomparable radiance of Thy eternal brightness bless Thee, and the golden loveliness of Thy dazzling beauty praise Thee.

Let the abyss of Thy just judgments bless Thee, and the unfathomable depths of Thy eternal wisdom praise Thee. Let the infinite treasures of Thy inexhaustible tenderness bless Thee, and the immense weight of all Thy mercies praise Thee.

3

Now offer unto the Lord a sacrifice of jubilation and say devoutly:

Let all the kindness of Thy love sing jubilantly unto Thee, and the limitless abundance of Thy infinite goodness. Let Thy boundless and overflowing charity towards men sing jubilantly unto Thee, and the measureless liberality of Thy bounteous love. Let the triumphant strength of Thy overflowing sweetness sing jubilantly unto Thee, and the plenitude of happiness which awaiteth all Thy loved ones in Thee.

4

Now adore the Lord God, begging that He will admit thee into His holy tabernacle, and that He will praise Himself on thy behalf; and say these words:

O Life most blessed, O my God, my gaze is fixed upon Thee alone! Oh when will a life-giving ray from Thee draw me, who am but the tiniest of sparks, unto Thee in the brightness of the saints,[28] that my tongue also may join in the jubilant praise which is offered unto Thee before Thy throne, where equal

28 Ps. 109:3.

praise is paid unto the Father, and unto the Son, and unto the Holy Ghost, by all Thy saints, in one blended hymn of thanksgiving? Oh when will my desires, like strings on the lyres of the seraphim, vibrate unceasingly before Thee in the ineffable chant of the trisagion, that the joy and jubilation of my heart may praise Thee in unison with the blessed who sing in Thy presence?

Oh when shall I be delivered from the snare of the hunters [29] and wrapped in the snow-white fleece of Thy purity, that I may see Thee, whose beauty surpasseth that of the countenances of the angels, leading the choirs of the virgins and of all the saints? When shall I hear the new canticle of the eternal nuptials, which Thou, O King and Bridegroom of the blessed, dost so harmoniously sing before them unto the music of Thy harp? This is the canticle wherein the glory of Thy beautiful voice resoundeth above all the instruments of heaven, while never a voice or tongue hath power to praise Thee as Thou shouldst be praised.

Oh how wondrous is the jubilation of paradise, where sovereign praise and thanksgiving are eternally offered unto the Lord, One in substance and Three in persons, by the very Unity and the very Trinity of God; where all the music of heaven husheth its beautiful strains in silence, and all the company of the seraphim fold their wings! Come, O God of my heart, my Beloved most dearly desired, in this sufficiency of praise which is Thine by reason of the infinite abundance of Thy Being, let Thy voice add at this hour, unto the hymn which riseth from Thy Divine Heart, a new strain of praise and thanksgiving on my behalf, unworthy as I am; and let the instrument of Thy jubilation pay homage unto Thee on my behalf for all the blessings which Thou hast bestowed upon me by creating me, by redeeming me, and by choosing me out of the world.

[29] Cf. Ps. 123:7.

And in that new strain of praise, inclose within Thyself my love by so sure a bond of affection that my heart, in its inmost being, may sing jubilantly unto Thee without ceasing, all the while that I endure this wretched exile. Let me ever thirst to praise Thee and long to return unto Thee who didst create me, until at length I lay aside the weight of this body and show myself in Thy presence. There in Thy heavenly sanctuary, my heart shall be filled with joy and my tongue with jubilation at the vision of Thy Divine countenance; there I will rejoice for evermore in Thy goodness and will exult in the eternal fruition of the glory of Thy face. Amen.

IV

Now as if thou wert entirely overwhelmed at the immensity of the riches and delights of the glory of thy God, at the incredible loveliness of His praise, at the glory of the angels and saints who stand in His presence, and at the sublime beauty of His resplendent and glorious countenance, do thou sing the canticle of the three young men in the fiery furnace, to invite all the creatures of God to praise Him:

DANIEL 3:57-88, 56

All ye works of the Lord, bless the Lord; praise and exalt Him above all for ever.

O ye angels of the Lord, bless the Lord; O ye heavens, bless the Lord.

O all ye waters that are above the heavens, bless the Lord; O all ye powers of the Lord, bless the Lord.

O ye sun and moon, bless the Lord; O ye stars of heaven, bless the Lord.

O every shower and dew, bless ye the Lord; O all ye spirits of God, bless the Lord.

O ye fire and heat, bless the Lord; O ye cold and heat, bless the Lord.

O ye dews and hoar frosts, bless the Lord; O ye frost and cold, bless the Lord.

O ye ice and snow, bless the Lord; O ye nights and days, bless the Lord.

O ye light and darkness, bless the Lord; O ye lightnings and clouds, bless the Lord.

O let the earth bless the Lord; let it praise and exalt Him above all for ever.

O ye mountains and hills, bless the Lord; O all ye things that spring up in the earth, bless the Lord.

O ye fountains, bless the Lord; O ye seas and rivers, bless the Lord.

O ye whales and all that move in the waters, bless the Lord; O all ye fowls of the air, bless the Lord.

O all ye beasts and cattle, bless the Lord; O ye sons of men, bless the Lord.

O let Israel bless the Lord; let them praise and exalt Him above all for ever.

O ye priests of the Lord, bless the Lord; O ye servants of the Lord, bless the Lord.

O ye spirits and souls of the just, bless the Lord; O ye holy and humble of heart, bless the Lord.

O Ananias, Azarias, and Misael, bless ye the Lord; praise and exalt Him above all for ever.

Let us bless the Father and the Son with the Holy Spirit; let us praise and exalt Him above all for ever.

Blessed art Thou, O Lord, in the firmament of heaven; and worthy of praise and glorious for ever.

1

Now thou shalt say:

My heart and my flesh have rejoiced in Thee, O living God,[30]

30 Cf. Ps. 83:3.

and my soul hath been glad in Thee, my true Saviour! How wonderful is Thy temple, O Lord, King of hosts! How glorious is Thy dwelling place, where Thou, O God most high, dost hold sway in Thy majesty over all things! My soul fainteth away with longing to enter the abode of Thy glory. O my God, Thou love and jubilation of my heart, my refuge and my strength, my glory and my praise, when shall my soul praise Thee in company with the saints? [31] When shall my eyes behold Thee, O my God, Thou God of gods? O God of my heart, when wilt Thou gladden me with the vision of Thy glorious face? Oh when wilt Thou grant me the desire of my soul and manifest Thy glory? O my God, Thou art my portion beyond all compare, my strength, and my glory! When shall I penetrate into Thy works of power,[32] that I may behold Thy might and Thy glory? [33] Oh when wilt Thou clothe me with the garment of praise rather than with the spirit of mourning, that my whole being may offer Thee a sacrifice of praise together with the angels?

O God of my life, when shall I enter into the tabernacle of Thy glory and join my voice unto the Alleluja that is sung before Thee in all its splendor, while my soul and heart praise Thee in the presence of all Thy saints, because of the great and countless mercies which Thou hast showered upon me? O my God, my dazzling inheritance, when will the snare of this mortal life be broken, and my soul be set free to praise Thee, beholding Thee without a veil? Oh when shall I dwell in Thy tabernacle for evermore, that I may praise Thy name unceasingly and sing unto Thy magnificence a new hymn, extolling Thy limitless mercies?

None is like unto Thee amongst the gods, O my Lord,[34] and naught can compare with the sublimity of the riches of Thy wondrous glory. Who shall sound the abyss of Thy wisdom,

[31] Cf. Ps. 149:1.   [32] Cf. Ps. 70:16.
[33] Cf. Ps. 62:3.   [34] Ps. 85:8.

and who shall number the infinite treasures of Thy boundless mercy? In truth, no greatness, no goodness can compare with Thine, O my God, Thou King immortal. Who shall unfold the glory of Thy majesty? Who can ever have his fill of the vision of Thy splendor? How shall the eye of man behold enough, or the ear of man hear enough, when he standeth before the awesome glory of Thy countenance?

O my God, Thou alone art wonderful and glorious. Thou alone art great and praiseworthy; Thou alone art kind and loveworthy; Thou alone art fair and lovely; Thou alone art beautiful and full of delights; Thou alone art He whose greatness, goodness, and glory are unrivalled whether in heaven or upon earth. Thy wondrous light is dearer unto my heart than the most far-flung glory; its beams alone can give joy unto my spirit and turn the irksomeness of this life into triumph and gladness.

Oh when wilt Thou light the lamp of my soul that it may nevermore go out, and kindle it anew in Thyself, causing me to know myself in Thee even as I am known?[35] Oh how blessed is the man who is already kept hidden in the glory of Thy countenance! Oh when will a ray of this glory absorb me too, unworthy as I am, that I may become one love and one spirit with Thee? My whole being crieth out unto Thee: "Lord, who is like unto Thee?"[36] Truly in glory Thou hast no equal, for Thou art the only God, glorious and exalted above all for ever. Oh when wilt Thou lift this poor little creature of Thine out of the dust, that I may stand before the face of Thy majesty, my head no longer covered with ashes but crowned with the diadem of eternal joy bestowed upon me by Thee? Then shall my soul sing Thy praises in eternal jubilation for all the favors which Thou hast granted me of Thy own free gift.

My soul and my heart already burn with desire for Thee, O

[35] Cf. 1 Cor. 13:12.   [36] Cf. Ps. 34:10.

God of my heart, O God who art my portion for ever! [37] My spirit rejoiceth in Thee, O God my Saviour! [38] If every created being were in my power, I would call upon all these beautiful works of Thy fingers [39] to praise and glorify Thee together. At the mere thought of Thy praise, my spirit and my soul begin to grow faint. If I had the strength of angels and men put together, I would gladly lavish it all upon praise of Thee, that I might know by experience those paeans of praise and of ineffable joy that rise before Thy sacred throne, where Thou dost keep Thy sabbath of beatific rest, Thou and the Ark of Thy holiness with Thee, and where thousands of thousands from the hosts of heaven sing before Thee day and night without ceasing: "Holy, Holy, Holy!"

There into the golden censer of Thy Divine Heart (where ever burneth in praise of Thee the exquisite perfume of eternal love), even I do cast a tiny grain of incense, which is nothing other than my own heart. I yearn and desire that this heart of mine, despite its meanness and unworthiness, may be quickened by the mighty breath of Thy Spirit and transmuted into pure fuel for Thy praise; and that the long sighs after Thee, which, because of my weary time of waiting, I send up from the abysmal depths of earth, may redound unto Thy everlasting praise and glory. Amen.

2

Then as if thou wert transported in spirit and soul with the desire to praise God, yet couldst find no words befitting His grandeur, pray unto the Lord Jesus, thy Lover, that He Himself would glorify Himself on Thy behalf with that sublime praise which befitteth Him, pleaseth Him, and giveth Him the greatest delight. Therefore do Thou say devoutly with thy heart and thy mouth:

[37] Ps. 72:26.   [38] Cf. Luke 1:47.   [39] Cf. Ps. 8:4.

The Exercises of Saint Gertrude

Blessed be Thou, O my God and my delight, by the sacred glory of Thy Godhead, wherewith Thou didst deign for nine months to dwell within the chaste womb of the Virgin Mary. Blessed be Thou by the sublime power of Thy Godhead, which stooped to the vale of the Virgin's lowliness. Blessed be Thou, O God most high, by Thy creative omnipotence, whereby Thou didst confer upon that virginal rose such virtue, loveliness, and beauty that Thou Thyself couldst find her delightsome.

Blessed be Thou by Thy marvellous wisdom, which lavished upon Mary so much grace that her body, her soul, and her whole life became worthy of the designs of Thy greatness. Blessed be Thou by Thy love, most strong, most wise, and most sweet, whereby Thou, the flower and Bridegroom of virginity, didst become the Virgin's Son. Blessed be Thou by the emptying of Thyself of Thy majesty, which hath won for me the treasures of an eternal inheritance. Blessed be Thou by Thy assuming of our humanity, which hath called me unto the partaking of Thy Godhead. Blessed be Thou by the exile which, for my sake, Thou didst suffer for the space of thirty-three years, that Thou mightest bring back my soul, which had been lost, unto the fountain of eternal life.

Blessed be Thou by all the labor, sorrow, and sweat of Thy Manhood, whereby Thou hast sanctified all my perplexities, anguish, and weariness. Blessed be Thou by the experience of my human misery which Thou didst undergo, whereby Thou wast made for me a Father of infinite mercy and a God of boundless clemency. Blessed be Thou by Thy inexhaustible love, whereby Thou Thyself didst become the priceless ransom of my soul. Blessed be Thou by each smallest drop of Thy precious blood, whereby Thou didst give life unto my soul and redeem me at so dear a price.

Blessed be Thou by the bitterness of Thy precious death, which Thy strong love brought upon Thee for my sake; because of its merits, I do not fear to take unto myself from Thee whatever merits are lacking in me, knowing with certainty that Thou truly carest for me, because Thou art mine and I am Thine by the eternal rights which Thou hast acquired over me. Blessed be Thou by Thy triumphal glory, wherewith in my human flesh Thou sittest at the right hand of the Father, for Thou art God, blessed for ever. Blessed be Thou by Thy own splendor, beauty, and power, which are the perfect happiness and marvelous feast of all the hosts of heaven.

3

Now as if thou wert cleaving with thy whole being unto God thy Lover, pray unto the Lord that He, with His dear Mother the Virgin Mary and the whole army of paradise, may offer unto Himself a sacrifice of jubilation, in the fair joyousness of His exquisite love; and that He Himself, the most skilled of harpists, may sing first upon the organ of His Godhead and then upon the harp of His Manhood. Therefore do thou say these words with thy heart and thy mouth:

O God of my life, let the Godhead of Thy ever-reigning Trinity, the Unity of Thy essence, the distinction of Thy Divine Persons, Their ineffable society, and Their incomparable mutual intimacy, sing jubilantly unto Thee on my behalf. Let Thy incomprehensible grandeur in all its sublimity, Thy immutable eternity, Thy unattainable purity, Thy ever-welling holiness, and Thy glorious and perfect felicity, sing jubilantly unto Thee. Let the most pure flesh of Thy Manhood, wherein Thou didst purify me, having been made bone of my bone and flesh of my flesh, sing jubilantly unto Thee.

Let Thy all-resplendent soul, that precious pledge whereby my soul hath been redeemed, sing jubilantly unto Thee. Let Thy Divine and most sweet Heart, which, in the hour of Thy death, love did pierce for my sake, sing jubilantly unto Thee. Let Thy most loving and most faithful Heart, into which the lance did open a way for me, that my heart might enter and rest therein, sing jubilantly unto Thee. Let this Heart most sweet, the sole refuge of my earthly sojourning, which ever watcheth over me with such kindness, and which will never rest in its thirst for me until it taketh me eternally unto itself, sing jubilantly unto Thee.

Let the incomparable heart and soul of the most glorious Virgin Mary, whom Thou didst choose as Thy Mother for my salvation and advantage, that her motherly clemency might ever avail me, sing jubilantly unto Thee. Let Thy most faithful watchfulness over me, whereby Thou hast provided me with so loving an advocate and patroness, through whom I may most easily find Thy grace, and in whom I confidently believe Thy eternal mercy is in store for me, sing jubilantly unto Thee. Let this same wondrous tabernacle of Thy glory, who alone hath served Thee worthily as a holy dwelling place, and through whom Thou canst best recover that measure of praise and glory which is my unpaid debt unto Thee, sing jubilantly unto Thee.

Let those seven glorious spirits who stand before Thy throne, sing jubilantly unto Thee on my behalf. Let the countless hosts of the holy angels, whom Thou dost send forth to minister unto the souls whom Thou hast chosen and redeemed, sing jubilantly unto Thee. Let the four and twenty elders, together with all the patriarchs and prophets, who fall down to worship Thee, casting their crowns before Thy throne and offering Thee infinite praise and thanksgiving upon their harps, sing jubilantly unto Thee. Let the four winged creatures, who celebrate Thy praise day and night with their whole being, sing jubilantly unto Thee.

Let the high office of the apostles, Thy dearest friends and brethren, by whose prayers Thou dost wondrously sustain holy Church, sing jubilantly unto Thee. Let the victorious company of the martyrs, empurpled with Thy precious blood, sing jubilantly unto Thee. Let the all-perfect army of the confessors, whose souls Thou hast transported into Thy wonderful light,[40] sing jubilantly unto Thee. Let the holy and spotless choirs of virgins, adorned with the snow-white brightness of a purity like unto Thine, sing jubilantly unto Thee. Let that new canticle which riseth from their lips as they follow Thee whithersoever Thou goest, O blessed Jesus, King and Bridegroom of virgins, sing jubilantly unto Thee. Let the sweetness of Thy Godhead and the ineffable banquet whereby the heavenly Jerusalem doth feast and find refreshment in the splendor of Thy Divine countenance, sing jubilantly unto Thee. Let the whole army of Thy elect, the inheritance chosen by Thee and the people set apart for Thyself, because they are with Thee, and Thou, their God, art with them for all eternity, sing jubilantly unto Thee.

Let all the stars of heaven, which shine before Thee with joy and are ever at hand, ready to obey Thy behests, sing jubilantly unto Thee. Let all Thy wonderful works which are held within the span of heaven, earth, and the abyss, sing jubilantly unto Thee; let them all sing that never-ending praise which, coming forth from Thee, returneth again unto Thee who art its beginning. Let my heart and soul, with the whole substance of my flesh and spirit, call upon the entire universe to join in singing jubilantly unto Thee.

Unto Thee, therefore, from whom are all things, through whom are all things, and in whom are all things, unto Thee alone be honor and glory for evermore! Amen.

4

Now as if thou wert somewhat refreshed and thy heart expanded from having praised Thy God and King, who dwelleth in His holy place, thou shalt rise up and find thy delight in God thy Lover. Deliver over unto Him all the love of Thy heart, that He may nourish thee with the blessings of

---

[40] 1 Pet. 2:9.

His sweetness [41] *and bring thee at last unto the blessing of enjoying Him fully and eternally in heaven. And say these words:*

O my God, because Thou art mine, I want for nothing.[42] And because I am Thine, I shall glory eternally in Thee, O God my Saviour. While I am plunged in sadness, Thou art preparing for me in Thyself the banquet which my soul desireth. And where shall my soul find happiness if not in Thee, O God of my life? If the thought of Thy praise is so sweet amid the miseries of this life, what will it be when Thy glory, O my God, is revealed in the splendor of Thy Godhead? If the foretaste of Thy sweetness bestowed drop by drop is so refreshing, what will it be, O Most Holy, when the plenitude of Thyself is given unto me? If the comfort which Thou dost impart unto me satisfieth my desire with good things here, what will it be when Thou, O God of my salvation, dost engulf my spirit in Thyself?

Oh what will be the pastures of that land where Thou dost show Thyself face to face, when even here my soul is so transported with delight at being admitted—all too seldom, alas! and for too short a time—unto the earthly pasture that giveth a taste of Thy delights! Oh what refreshment will be mine in the presence of Thy Divine countenance, when even here the inmost being of my spirit and soul is so richly nourished at the waters where Thou dost offer me the refreshment of Thy hidden consolations! O my God, when Thou convertest my soul unto Thee, Thou dost not suffer me to think or to feel aught apart from Thee; Thou takest me away from myself in Thee, that I may have no anxiety for myself, because Thou hast hidden me from myself in Thee.

And then what joy, rejoicing, and jubilation will be mine, when Thou revealest unto me the beauty of Thy Godhead, and

[41] Cf. Ps. 20:4.   [42] See Ps. 22.

my soul beholdeth Thee face to face! Surely in that hour, with deepest gladness, I shall be still and behold Thy glory, O God; I shall draw near the altar whereon my reconciliation unto Thee was accomplished, and I shall offer up unto Thee the inmost being of my soul in jubilation and praise.

Then, O my soul, thou shalt see, and thou shalt receive gifts in profusion, and thy heart shall marvel and open wide, when the vast riches, delights, and magnificence of the glory of that broad ocean which is the ever-adorable Trinity shall turn towards thee; when the strength of the nations, which the King of Kings and Lord of Lords [43] by His strong hand hath redeemed from the hand of the enemy, shall come unto thee; and when the flood of God's mercy and charity, omnipotence, and wisdom and bounty shall cover thee,[44] bestowing upon thee the dignity of the Divine adoption for all eternity. Then shall be given unto thee the chalice of the beatific vision even unto drunkenness, the goodly inebriating chalice of the glory of the Divine countenance; and thou shalt drink of the torrent of the delights of God,[45] when He, the very fountain of light, shall refresh thee eternally in the raptures of His plenitude. Then shalt thou behold the heavens full of the glory of God who maketh them His dwelling place; thou shalt see that Virginal luminary, who, after God, enlighteneth all paradise with the brightness of her all-pure light; and thou shalt gaze upon the wonderful works of the fingers of God, and the morning stars [46] who rejoice to stand before the face of God and minister unto Him.

O God of my heart, whom I have so happily chosen as my inheritance, alas! how much longer is my soul to be debarred from the presence of Thy longed-for countenance? Thou alone knowest the full tale of miseries which I endure in my sojourn-

---

[43] 1 Tim. 6:15.
[44] See Isai. 60:5-6.
[45] Cf. Ps. 35:9.
[46] Job. 38:7.

ing upon earth, all my fraility, and the irksomeness of my life of exile.

Come, O Beloved, for whom I have yearned so long, the inmost depths of my heart do thirst for Thee. Come speedily and bring me unto Thee, O God, Thou living fountain, that in Thee I may drink of eternal life for evermore. Come speedily and let Thy face shine upon me, that I may with joy behold Thee face to face. Come speedily and show me Thyself, that I may rejoice in Thee in eternal felicity.

Come, O Life of my spirit, do Thou transform the cry of my desire and join it in one single voice with the festive song of Thy love. Take possession of my life, and fix my soul so immutably in Thy love that all my life and all my deeds may sing Thy praises on the ten-stringed lyre, and all my intentions, united unto Thee, may begin, keep on, and end in Thee, O Thou true Life of my soul!

Come, O true Love of my heart, in this hour do Thou on my behalf give glory unto Thyself, with praise and thanksgiving of such solemnity and splendor that all the choirs of heaven may join the hymn; for Thou Thyself, O my God, art unto me the all-surpassing and the sweetest Good; and though I am the least of all Thy creatures, yet wouldst Thou have me acknowledge, love, and praise Thee, for Thou art God my Saviour, the one Author of my salvation, and the Life of my soul.

And in this solemnity of praise, let my soul pour forth upon Thee all the meagre resources of my spirit, fainting away with love of Thy praise, until my spirit happily returneth unto Thee, O God! And do Thou give me in this life such delight in the thought of Thy praise, that, at the hour of my death, my thirst and strong love to behold Thee, to praise Thee, and to be with Thee may overcome in me the violence of death, and Thou Thyself in that anguish mayest be my door and my homeland, bringing me at last unto the untold bliss of the life of heaven, that my spirit and my soul may rejoice in Thee eternally. Amen.

V

Now like a solitary turtledove, pining away with weariness of this life in thy eagerness to behold the glorious face of the Beloved, fold the wings of thy desires, like unto the four living creatures before God's throne.[47]

1

Then thou shalt declare, in the presence of the Lord Thy God, that where He, thy longed-for treasure is, there thy whole heart is also,[48] *and beseech Him to grant thee a happy death:*

My heart hath fixed itself unto the will of Jesus, who is my Life. Come, O Jesus, Thou who art beloved above all other loves, Thou art the faithful Life of my soul. Only for Thee doth my soul faint away; only for Thee doth my heart secretly thirst. Thy beatitude with all its delights, Thy marvellous loveliness, Thy adorable countenance, Thy beauty demanding all my love, have inflicted upon me a delicious wound which maketh it burdensome unto me to behold the daylight of this world.

I am weary of myself. How long, O my Beloved, must I wait before I can attain the joy that is in Thee and the contemplation of Thy most lovable face? My soul is athirst for Thee. Without Thee, heaven and earth and everything they hold seem unto me like the frost of winter. Thy most lovable face is my single comfort, my solace, and my springtide. O Love, when wilt Thou do me the favor of destroying my body, that it may return unto dust and my soul flow back into Thee, O God, its living Source? The pure light of Thy glory, which shineth forth from Thy celestial throne in Divine rays of love, hath utterly pervaded my spirit. Why should a poor little leaf wait longer on the tree in the midst of the tempest of this world?

Come, O Love, hold me with Thy strong right hand, lest my

---

[47] See Apoc. 4:8.   [48] Cf. Matt. 6:21.

soul should be submerged in that tempest. The musical sound of the living water gushing out from its Divine Source hath powerfully taken possession of my heart; never a lyre did sound such music. This life hath become for me as shadowy as a dream; how much longer must I suffer its illusion?

Come, o LOVE, loose me never from thy bond, until thou hast presented me unto the sole Beloved of my heart and brought me unto the bosom of the Lord. O my best Beloved, Thou lovely fragrance of the fruit of life which is Thyself, Thou hast taken away my spirit from me, so that my body seemeth unto me a putrid and repulsive thing, wherefore I never cease to sigh after Thee.

Come, o LOVE, when wilt thou set me free from this body, that I may have the fruition of my heart's Beloved without a veil and abide with Him world without end? One single ray of Thy Godhead, bestowed upon me through Thy Manhood, doth impart such surpassing joy unto my spirit that, had I a thousand bodies, I would promptly despise them. Tell me then, what delights shall I experience when I attain unto the fruition of Thy splendor, grown at last transparent? A thousand deaths would I die and count it nothing, might I but contemplate Thy truth in all its sweetness.

Come, o LOVE, deal mercifully with me and take me up speedily to that magnificent festival, where I shall contemplate the glory of the faithful Saviour who is my Bridegroom. Only the plenitude of Thy Godhead can satisfy my soul, which Thou hast deigned to create for Thyself. When I drink in one single drop of Thy sweetness, my spirit is so strongly seized with rapture that death taketh on for me the taste of life, for by it I shall come to contemplate Thy face unceasingly.

Come, O Love, when wilt Thou so separate my soul and body that my spirit may dwell continually in Thee, who art unto me most dear? Thy loving embrace giveth such a taste of sweetness that, had I a thousand hearts, they would all melt in an instant. Thy ardent kiss, instinct with life, sinketh in Thee my life and strongly bindeth unto Thee my soul. How gladly would I draw my last breath, that I might fully penetrate into the flood of Thy Godhead!

O Love, wilt Thou not finally celebrate within me the festival of Thy nuptials, that my soul, escaping from this vale of wretchedness, may be engulfed in its Source, like a drop of water in the sea? Come, O dearest Jesus, Thou whom my heart supremely loveth and prefereth, be Thou my guide in this wretched exile, that in praise of Thee I may end my days and in Thy grace and friendship happily finish my life.

Come, Jesus, dear Love, be Thou a refuge for Thy poor bride, who, apart from Thee, owneth naught and possesseth naught that is good. Do Thou direct her course upon the vast sea of this world and comfort her in the fearful tempest of death. Reach out unto me the hand of Thy compassion, and be Thou Thyself the staff of my strength, whereon I may lean so securely, O dear deliverer of my soul, that all the treachery and insolence of my enemies may, at the sight of Thy power, be brought to naught.

Come, Jesus, my faithful friend, let the abyss of Thy inexhaustible mercy be for me a safe harbor, wherein I may escape from the fierce insults of all my enemies. And in that hour be Thou Thyself a place of sanctuary for me, whither I may fly with joyful haste, to be freed from the captivity of all my wrongdoing. Come, Jesus, my dear hope, let Thy Divine Heart, wounded for love of me and open at every hour unto all sinners, be the first refuge of my soul when it leaveth my body. In this abyss of Thy infinite love, let all my sins be devoured in an instant, that I may be rid of every hindrance and enter with Thee, O Beloved of my heart, into the joys of heaven.

Come, Jesus, my sole salvation, my Saviour and my God, in my last hour send me Thy most loving Mother Mary, the radiant star of the sea, to be my faithful helper, that at the sight of the golden dawn of her glorious face, I may know that Thou, O Sun of Justice, in the brightness of Thy light, art drawing near unto my soul. Come, O my Beloved, above all who are beloved, Thou knowest the desire of my heart, for my soul sigheth after Thee alone. Make haste, therefore, and come, that in the presence of Thy beauteous countenance I may utterly forget all the sorrows of my heart.

Come, O Love, keep a close watch over the hour of my death and impress Thy seal upon it, that under Thy sure protection and through Thy surpassing bounty (whereon I place all my reliance), nothing may have power to harm my soul. At the time of my passing, show me Thy benign wisdom and console my wretched soul so perfectly that for all eternity it may be aureoled with the surpassing mercy which Thou, O King of glory, hast wrought in it through Thyself, both in my life and in my death. Then in Thy might consume all my strength and through Thy mercy submerge me in the abyss of Thy Godhead; there may the face of Jesus, the Beloved of my heart, satisfy me, revivify me, and enrich me in Thy glory. Amen.

2

Now commend unto God once more thy death and the end of thy life, that He may be thy Helper in all things and may order and dispose the end of thy life according to His mercy. Therefore recite this prayer:

My God and my Lord, my beloved Creator and Redeemer, in whom my heart hath placed all its hope, in whom I have believed, whom I have confessed, O Thou verdant flower of the Godhead, sprinkle me over with the dew of Thy flower-laden Manhood, that my soul may rejoice under the dewdrops of Thy holy charity and meekness, forgetting the woes of this earthly exile, and putting forth more and more the buds of all virtues in Thee, O Thou sovereign Bud and Flower of all virtues, bearing calmly with Thee the miseries of this sojourning upon earth, and exercising patience in all tribulation and distress.

My God and my King, who art in Thy holy place, in whom my life is hidden with my Jesus,[49] behold, the deluge of Thy chaste delights hath flowed over me. I am already lost unto myself in Thee, and living, I have died. And now where shall I go to leave Thee? Whether in heaven or on earth, I now know nothing save Thee. O my God, Thou who art praised by Israel, Thou who dwellest in Thy holy place,[50] Thou in whom I have my being, Thou in whom I move and live,[51] all my trust is in Thee. In Thee doth my heart open wide, for Thou alone art all my joy and all that I desire. The ray of Thy light hath awakened my soul from its slumber.

Oh when will my soul be engulfed in the river of life, in the rapturous waters of the eternal fruition of Thee? Oh when will the flood of Thy love carry away my spirit and bring me unto Thee, that I may behold Thy glorious countenance, O God of my life, Thou Author of my salvation and Helper of my soul, without whom I am nothing, know nothing, can do nothing, and count for nothing, in whom is all my hope, unto whom I long to come, whose life-giving face with all its delights I am eager to behold, and unto whom I yearn, with my whole heart, my whole soul, and my whole strength, to be united without fear of loss for all eternity?

Come, do Thou consecrate my being and my life solely unto Thy praise and unto Thy glory, that my inmost soul in its every thought, word, deed, and impulse, together with the whole strength and substance of my body, may praise and glorify Thee in the fulness of charity and love. Behold how my soul must sojourn in the prison of this body, while it ardently desireth, burneth, and longeth for Thee, O God, the fountain of life! Behold how wretched I am in this exile, knowing neither its beginning nor its ending! And behold, above all, how Thou, O

---

[49] See Col. 3:3.   [50] Cf. Ps. 21:4.   [51] See Acts 17:28.

Father of mercies, dost neither forsake nor despise the work of Thy hands! [52] Let these reasons stir the abyss of Thy mercy, and look Thou upon my earthly sojourning with that same loving mercy wherewith Thou didst have pity upon me, when for thirty-three years Thou didst deign to experience this same exile; and with that same compassion which Thou hadst for me when Thou didst redeem me upon the cross and Thy most sweet Heart was broken by love.

Come, O Thou most blessed Life of my soul, in all my temptations be Thou my triumph and my victory; in all weaknesses, be Thou my patience; in every tribulation, be Thou my comfort; in all thoughts, words, and works, be Thou my whole intention, my beginning, end, and perfection; in all my life, be Thou my sanctification; in the forbearance of my long days of waiting, even unto the end of the good fight, be Thou my perseverance.

Come, O Thou who art my glorious inheritance, whom my soul hath chosen as its best part, whom alone I await, in whom alone I hope! In the hour of my death do Thou dispose and order in Thy compassion and clemency all that befalleth me. Let the banner of Thy precious cross be unto me then a strong defence against all the wiles of Satan; and let the most noble arms of Thy victorious passion—the nails and the lance—be my sure weapons against his countless deceptions. Make Thy triumphant death of love a rampart round about me; sign me with Thy precious blood, the price of my redemption; and be Thou my Guide and my Viaticum, that I may pass in safety through the narrow gate of death.

And now, O my Salvation, leave me not, but appear unto me in Thy charity, compassion, and mercy, that I may behold Thee face to face, O my God, my Lover, who didst create me for Thyself. There, O dearest Jesus, Thou Helper of my soul, show me in the mirror of unveiled contemplation of Thyself,

[52] Cf. Ps. 137:8.

the glory of Thy Godhead, that my spirit and my soul may be filled with praise of Thee in all joy and splendor, and my heart may rejoice for evermore in Thee, O my dearest Saviour.

And then my soul, which Thou hast redeemed, will rejoice in the good things of Thy house; it will draw its inmost sustenance from the joy of the vision of Thy glorious face. It will be overwhelmed with happiness and gladness, because it hath escaped the endless wiles and snares of the devil, the flesh, and the world, together with the anguish of death; and because it possesseth Thee, who art my incomparable portion and my delightsome Life. Then in paradise Thou wilt be in me, and I in Thee, cleaving unto Thee with eternal and deathless love; and mindful of all the blessings which Thou hast bestowed upon me, I shall praise Thy name without ceasing, for Thou art the God of my life, the Redeemer and Lover of my soul.

3

Now ask the Lord to impart unto Thee His blessing and to confirm thee in His love, until thou shalt attain unto the vision of Him in heaven:

O unitive Love, O God of my heart, O Thou whom my spirit loveth and praiseth with jubilation! My King and my God! [53] My Beloved, whom I have chosen from among thousands! [54] All-lovely Bridegroom of my soul! O Lord, King of hosts, who art all the love, affection, and desire of my heart! Come, O Love, O God, be Thou in this world Thyself my blessed dower, my plenitude of Divine sweetness. Let my spirit cleave unto Thee in one same spirit, one same breath, one same will, one same charity, until this my spirit becometh one spirit with Thee for all eternity. O burning Love, be Thou Thyself unto me a blessing living and effectual, to urge me gently onward during my earthly pilgrimage, that my soul and all my strength and

[53] Ps. 5:3.   [54] Cf. Cant. 5:10.

[141]

substance may burn and never be extinguished, as a true spark in the flame of Thy charity.

O living Love, be Thou Thyself unto me a blessing perfective and conclusive, to present my soul unto Thee Thyself as a worthy bride, that by Thy charity my whole life may be governed, and my death in Thee, O my most blessed Life, may, in the full vigor of faith, hope, and charity, be perfectly consummated and, by all the sacraments of holy Church, worthily provided. Then all my powers being worn out in Thy service, and my bodily forces withered in Thy love, my soul, casting off the weight of the body, shall be free to follow Thee, O my kindest Lover, safe and rejoicing, unto the mysterious depths of the riches and beauty of the most holy Trinity. There, since all my sins have been forgiven by Thy compassion and all my offences buried in Thy inestimable charity, my poor lost life with all its ruins shall be restored by Thee, O richest Love, through the all-perfect life of Jesus my Lord. There my soul, which here on earth was drooping and wasting away through the weariness of this life, shall grow young again in Thee, O living Love; renewed like the eagle,[55] it shall exult with gladness and rejoice in the glory of Thy face, because it now hath found and holdeth in all security the infinite joys of everlasting life, which it will possess in Thee, O Love, O God, throughout eternity! Amen.

[55] Cf. Ps. 102:5.

7th Exercise

ATONEMENT FOR SIN
AND PREPARATION FOR DEATH

Commentary

To BE truly prepared for death, Gertrude teaches us, means being fully reconciled with God. We must therefore beseech the Father to forgive all our sins through the merits of the passion of Christ. She begins by apostrophizing Divine LOVE and bids us take this LOVE as our "ambassador" to appease the Father for us. She then goes on to personify other Divine perfections—MERCY, TRUTH, PEACE, WISDOM, Divine PREDILECTION, and COMPASSION—together with PERSEVERANCE, envisaged as Christ's persevering charity—and tells us that they will be our "advocates" with God.[1]

We are now to present ourself before the Father seven times, accompanied by our ambassador and each of our seven advocates successively. Thus Gertrude arranges what we may call seven scenes, which form a sequence like that in the fifth Exercise, corresponding to the seven Hours of the Divine Office. Naturally she avails herself here of the widespread medieval custom of matching the canonical Hours with the stages of Christ's passion, which she uses also in the *Herald*.[2] According to this familiar scheme, Matins (sung by Benedictines about two o'clock in the morning) was associated with the seizure of Christ in the garden of Gethsemani; Prime (at about six o'clock), with the mockery in the palace of the high priest; Terce (about nine o'clock), with the condemnation by Pilate;

[145]

Sext (at noon), with the crucifixion; None (at about three), with the piercing of Christ's side by the lance; Vespers (before sunset), with the taking down from the cross; and Compline (in the evening), with the entombment.

Gertrude's eloquent colloquies in these seven scenes may impress the reader first of all by their dramatic effect. But still more telling is their penetration into the sufferings and the love of Christ. Here he will catch the echo of her rapt meditations on the passion; as he turns the pages, he will find himself admitted for a little time to the holy of holies of a saint's heart. Among the many unforgettable passages, those on the death of Christ (under the hour of None) attain to an extraordinary pathos and sublimity.

These seven scenes, which we have called Part I, make up the greater portion of the seventh Exercise. The remaining pages divide themselves into two short sections. The first of these, Part II, is a series of seven prayers, all of similar construction, in which the sufferings of Christ are once more brought in contact with the daily needs of the spiritual life.[3] In the fourth of these prayers occurs a last mention of the wound of love (another was made in Part I under the hour of Terce). In the sixth prayer, we meet with an allusion of particular significance when Saint Gertrude addresses our Lord as "youth all-lovely," *juvenis amabilis*. The context seems to supply no special reason for the use of this expression; but there can hardly be any doubt that she is looking back to her first vision, in the account of which written by her own hand she says that Christ appeared to her that night as "a youth all-lovely," *juvenem amabilem*. This would seem to give added weight to the fact that in the last few lines of the seventh Exercise Gertrude refers to her heart as a "thorny thicket," evidently still thinking of the same vision and the hedge of thorns.[4]

Part III brings the entire book briefly and powerfully to a close, with a reminiscence of the petitions for the various virtues found in the liturgical prayers of the consecration. As the book of the *Exercises* begins with the prayer for God's blessing and the renewal of our heart, so it ends with a triple request for His blessing. The last prayer, which Gertrude places on our lips makes us request that our heart may ever abide with Christ, and His love with us, so that His blessing may be upon our death, and our soul may straightway find its eternal rest in Him.

7th Exercise

ATONEMENT FOR SIN
AND PREPARATION FOR DEATH

I

When thou dost wish to set apart a day for atonement, at each of the seven Hours thou must withdraw completely within thyself in recollection, in order to hold converse with LOVE. *Appoint this* LOVE *as thy ambassador unto the Father of mercies,[1] as if to appease Him, that out of the treasure of the passion of His Son He may forgive thee all thy debt, down to the very last point which thou hast not heeded. Then at thy death thou shalt have full confidence that all thy sins have been entirely forgiven thee.*

1

Begin therefore at Matins and recite the first strophe of this hymn:

> O Thou who dost liberally grant pardon,
> Lift up the love of our souls unto Thee;
> Show Thy clemency towards our hearts
> And purify them of their uncleanness.

[1] 2 Cor. 1:3.

Be Thou swayed by Thy compassion and put an end unto our woes by Thy pardon! In spite of my unworthiness, hear my request and satisfy me at the hour of death with the immediate vision of Thy sweet countenance, that I may have eternal rest in Thee.

And now, in company with MERCY *and* LOVE, *thou shalt appease the Father, saying with thy heart and thy lips these words:*

O sweet MERCY of God, full of compassion and clemency, behold, in my wretchedness and in the sorrow and distress of my heart, I flee unto thee for counsel, for thou art all my hope and all my trust. Thou hast never despised any poor wretch; thou hast never repulsed the foulest sinner. Thou hast never driven away him who fled unto thee; thou hast never passed by a person in distress without taking pity upon him. Thou hast ever been ready, like a mother, to help them who were in need; faithful unto thy name, thou hast stood beside all who invoked thee. Come, in spite of my unworthiness, cast me not away from thee by reason of my sins; repulse me not by reason of my unprofitable life!

Despise me not! Say not of me: "Why doth she still encumber the ground?" [2] Nay, with the pity which belongeth unto thy very nature, concern thyself with me. Behold, in my desperate lack of merits, lest I die under the open sky of the cold and rain of my fruitless life, I present myself at that all-charitable hospice for the poor which is in thee, hoping to receive from thy generous hand an alms whereby to retrieve my poor lost life. There with the fleecy sheepskins of thy tenderness, thou wilt bring back warmth unto my naked limbs, that by thy charity all my sins may be covered and all my heedlessness atoned for. Come, admit me into the security of thy dwelling, that I may be saved there by thy favor. Do thou obtain for me

2 See Luke 13:7.

the help of the tender charity of God, for by no other means shall my soul and spirit find health.

Come, O LOVE, turn thy gaze upon my Jesus, that royal Captive of thine, crowned with the diadem of mercy, whom thou didst seize at this hour with such violence, in order to lay claim not only unto Himself but unto all His goods, and thus to enrich heaven and earth by this inestimable booty of thine, filling all creatures with blessings from the abundance of thy most glorious Captive.

Come, with this precious booty, with this Captive immeasurably beloved, ransom for me my poor lost life, and restore unto me not seven times but a hundred times the value of my unprofitable deeds. Did I alone possess the being of all men and of all angels put together, this would still fall short of the worth of this incomparable Captive of thine; how much less, seeing that I am but a poor human creature of dust and ashes?

Oh had I but my choice! Then I would share the lot of my beloved Jesus, and thou shouldst take me also captive, little and weak as I am; thou shouldst bind me and hold me also in custody. Sharing the company and hearing the words of that Divine Captive, I should be changed from a sinner into a saint; from an idler, into a truly spiritual person; from an enemy of God, into His true friend; from a languid seeker after God, into one truly athirst for Him; from a sterile and fruitless soul, into one bringing forth all the perfect virtues and all the holiness of monastic life! O dearest Jesus, let the bosom of Thy mercy be the prison of my captivity. There let the chains of Thy Divine Heart be my fetters, and in the vehemence of Thy living love let me become Thy eternal captive, deathlessly united with Thee, living for Thee, and cleaving unto Thee, that I may nevermore be separated from Thee. Amen.

2

At the hour of Prime, hold converse with LOVE *and* TRUTH, *that they may speak for thee at the hour of death; then thou shalt come unto the judgment without fear, for thou wilt have as thy loving advocate none other than Jesus thy Judge Himself. Now therefore recite this next strophe:*

> O most gracious Lord,
> Thou knowest that man is a fallen creature;
> Our flesh is weak,
> And we live in constant wretchedness.

Be Thou swayed by Thy compassion and put an end unto our woes by Thy pardon! In spite of my unworthiness, hear my request and satisfy me at the hour of death with the immediate vision of Thy sweet countenance, that I may have eternal rest in Thee.

Now seek to appease God by this prayer:

O beloved TRUTH, O just equity of God, how shall I appear before thy face, laden as I am with my iniquity, with the guilt of having ruined my life, and with the burden of my persistent heedlessness? Most true it is that a fortune was placed in my hands when I was given the Christian faith and spiritual life; but I, alas! did not deposit it in the bank of charity, that it might be restored unto thee, according to thy wishes, with the rich interest of perfection. The talent of time which was intrusted unto me, I have squandered; worse than this, I have let it fall to the ground and lost it irrecoverably. Whither shall I go? Whither shall I turn? And whither shall I fly to escape from before thy face? [3]

O TRUTH, two impartial assessors—justice and equity—are thy waiting maids. Thou dost judge all things by number, weight, and measure.[4] Whatever cometh into thy hand, thou dost weigh upon thy unerring balance. Woe is me, should I be placed in thy power without an advocate to answer for me!

---

[3] Cf. Ps. 138:7.   [4] Cf. Wisd. 11:21.

O CHARITY, do thou offer entreaties for me! Answer thou for me, obtain my pardon, and plead my cause, that thanks to thee I may not lose my life.

I know what I will do. I will take the chalice of salvation.[5] I will set the chalice of Jesus in TRUTH's empty scalepan. Thus shall I atone for all that I lack and cover all my sins. By this chalice I shall fill in all the gaps in my ruins; by this chalice I shall more than atone for all my imperfections.

Come, O LOVE, give me my Jesus, that royal Captive of thine, whose tenderness is inwardly moved by the impulse of thy mercy. This is the hour wherein with such violence thou didst drag Him to judgment, that thou mightst lay upon Him the sins of the whole world and mine in particular, to exact of Him punishment for them, whereas He was without stain and bore this injustice only for love of me. Come, give Him unto me today to accompany me unto my judgment; let me receive Him from thee, O dearest LOVE, in all His dear innocence, condemned for love of my love and sentenced unto death for my sake. Give Him unto me as surety, that I may have Him as defender during all my trial.

O dearest TRUTH! To appear before thee without my Jesus, I would find intolerable; but how lovely and pleasant it is to come before thee in company with Him! Now, O TRUTH, seat thyself on thy tribunal; enter thy audience chamber now, and bring forth against me what accusations thou wilt. I shall have no fear of evil things;[6] I know that thy aspect will never put me to shame, since He who is all my hope and confidence will be with me. Tell me, what sentence wilt thou now pronounce against me, since I shall have my dearest Jesus with me? He is most faithful, and He hath borne my misery that He may obtain from thee unstinted mercy for me.

My sweetest Jesus, beloved pledge of my redemption, come Thou with me unto the judgment. Come, let us stand together.

5 Ps. 115:13.   6 Ps. 22:4.

Be Thou my Judge and my Advocate. Recount what Thou didst become for my sake, what solicitude Thou didst have for me, at what great cost Thou didst purchase me, all for my justification through Thee. Thou didst live for me, that I might not die. Thou didst bear my sins. Thou didst die for me, to save me from eternal death. Thou didst give me all that was Thine, that through Thee I might become rich in merits. At the hour of death, do Thou judge me according to that innocence and stainlessness which Thou hast conferred upon me in Thee, since all my debt hath been paid through Thee. Thou wast judged and condemned for my sake, that I, who of myself am only a poor beggar maid, might have all blessings in abundance through Thee.

3

At the hour of Terce, address thyself unto PEACE *and* LOVE, *begging them to consecrate thy understanding and thy thoughts unto the Lord for ever, that in the hour of death thou mayest be found fully reconciled unto God. Now therefore recite this next strophe:*

> Thou knowest of what we stand accused;
> No soul hath secrets from Thee.
> Rid us of all the idle fancies
> Of the deceitful world.

Be Thou swayed by Thy compassion and put an end unto our woes by Thy pardon! In spite of my unworthiness, hear my request and satisfy me at the hour of death with the immediate vision of Thy sweet countenance, that I may have eternal rest in Thee.

O PEACE of God, thou dost surpass all understanding;[7] thou art fair and lovable, sweet and venerable! Wherever thou comest, security sitteth undisturbed. Thou alone canst restrain

---

[7] Cf. Phil. 4:7.

the Sovereign's wrath; thou dost adorn the King's throne with clemency; thou dost enhance with compassion and mercy the kingdom where He reigneth in glory. Here I stand arraigned and poor; come, plead my cause. Come, shelter me under thy wings, that I may be protected there [8] from the woes which threaten and affright me because of my past heedlessness.

Behold, now the creditor standeth at my door, demanding back the life which I had received as a deposit in trust. The tax gatherer asketh of me the stated payment of the time that had been given me; and I cannot speak unto him with impunity, for I have naught wherewith to pay my debt. O dearest Jesus, Thou who art my peace,[9] how long wilt Thou be silent? How long wilt Thou dissemble and refrain from speech? Now at least speak for me, and in Thy charity say but this: "I will redeem her!" For Thou art the refuge of the wretched; Thou passest no one by without a greeting; Thou never hast dismissed unreconciled one who fled unto Thee for succor. Come, pass me not by in my misery and despair, without some sign of charity. Do Thou appease the Father for me; receive me in the bosom of Thy charity; give me to drink a cup of the cold water of holy hope, that I may live. O God of charity, do Thou cool my tongue. Do Thou restore life unto my soul, which is now ready to faint from spiritual want.

Come, O LOVE, this is the hour wherein for me my Jesus was scourged, crowned with thorns, and pitilessly ill-used. This is the hour wherein thou madest my true, my only King the reproach of men, abject, and despised like a leper, that Judea might reject Him, but I, thanks unto thee, might accept Him. For me my Jesus, having stolen naught, repaid the whole. Oh then, give Him unto me in all His innocence, that my soul may embrace Him! O let me receive Him upon my heart and revivify my spirit by the bitterness of His sorows and sufferings! Most bitter was the chastisement of my peace which thou didst

[8] See Ps. 16:8.   [9] See Eph. 2:14.

[154]

lay upon Him; may it be the quittance of all my debts and all my heedlessness.

O PEACE, be thou my glorious chain and bind me unto Jesus eternally. Be thou the cherished pillar of my strength, that being made fast unto thee by deathless friendship, I may become one heart and soul with Jesus. Thus in thee, O dearest PEACE, shall I sustain the scourges of charity, the inward wounds of love; through thee shall I remain eternally united unto my Jesus. O PEACE, grant me yet one small favor: open for me that alabaster box, that precious treasure of love which is in thy keeping, that the living fragrance thereof may arouse my spirit from its torpor.

Do thou bedew and anoint my members with the blood of that most glorious Head and with the suffering felt by His sacred members, that by this ineffable perfume I may be wholly transformed from cowardice and torpor of spirit, as in springtide the sterility of the earth is changed into a profusion of new flowers.

O my dearest Jesus, I pray Thee let the sufferings endured by Thy sacred members be the remission of all my sins and the atonement for all my heedlessness; that whatever is wanting in me, I may find in Thee, who didst spend Thyself utterly for me. Amen.

4

At the hour of Sext, hold converse with WISDOM *and* LOVE, *that thy whole inner being may be renewed, and that in the hour of thy death, thou mayest be defended by the power of the precious cross of Christ from every temptation and the wiles of the enemy. Now therefore recite this next strophe:*

> We came hither as strangers,
> And we groan in our exile;
> Thou art our port and our homeland;
> Bring us unto the courts of eternal life.

Be Thou swayed by Thy compassion and put an end unto our woes by Thy pardon! In spite of my unworthiness, hear my request and satisfy me at the hour of death with the immediate vision of Thy sweet countenance, that I may have eternal rest in Thee.

O marvellous WISDOM of God, how powerful and glorious is thy voice! All who desire thee, thou callest unto thee. Thou makest thy dwelling in the humble; thou lovest them who love thee.[10] Thou dost judge the poor man's cause; thou art kind and merciful unto all alike. Thou hatest nothing of what thou hast created.[11] Thou makest semblance of not beholding the sins of men, while in thy mercy thou dost wait for them to do penance.[12] Come, open unto me also the fountain of life and let me drink the cup of thy indulgence, that I may know what is pleasing in thy sight [13] at all seasons.

O WISDOM, thou bearest in thy right hand the sacred banner of eternity; with thee is the happy issue of all things. Thou only and thou alone canst do all things. Immutable in thyself, thou dost renew all things. Come, renew and sanctify me in thee, that thou mayest take up thy dwelling in my soul. It is thou who dost make men the friends of God; come, obtain the friendship of God for me. Impel me early in the morning to keep watch before thee,[14] that in truth I may find thee. Come forth to meet me, that in truth I may desire thee.

With what prudence thou dost direct thy ways! With what providence thou dost dispose all things, thou who, for man's salvation, didst seek with most prudent counsel to win over the King of glory! Thou didst whisper thoughts of peace, drawing His awesome majesty unto the designs of thy charity; thou didst lay upon His back the burden of love, that He might bear the iniquity of the people upon the tree.[15] O glorious WISDOM of God, all the malice of the devil could not hinder thy magnificent

10 Cf. Prov. 8:17. 11 Wisd. 11:25. 12 Cf. *ibid.* 11:24.
13 Cf. *ibid.* 9:10. 14 Cf. Isai. 26:9. 15 Cf. 1 Pet. 2:24.

works; all the ignorance of human perversity could not alter thy merciful counsels; all the magnitude of our crimes could not prevail against the wealth of thy mercies, the immensity of thy love, and the plenitude of thy bounty! Thy sovereign design it was that won the day and ordered all things sweetly, reaching from end unto end mightily.[16]

Thou, o WISDOM, art the all-excelling strength of the Divine majesty; oh that in me, unworthy as I am, thou wouldst show thy efficacy! Oh that in me, contemptible as I am, by the Holy Spirit, that Breath of thy mouth, thou wouldst throw down all barriers to thy will and good pleasure! Thus through thee shall I conquer all temptations; in the greatness of love, I shall die unto myself and live through thee; I shall surmount all obstacles in thee. Thanks then to thy guidance, I shall escape from the shipwreck of this life, for I shall receive from thee charity as my covering and affection as my garment, and seal with thee the covenant of a living love.

Ah, WISDOM, what a game thou playest, how thou dost circumvent my Jesus! Thou dost strip the King of glory, to make Him a spectacle of ignominy. Thou dost nail unto the cross the whole world's Ransom. Thou alone dost weigh and mark out the worth of this mystery which payeth the debt of all transgression. Thou dost lift up from the earth upon the cross the Life of all men, that by His death He may draw all things unto Himself [17] and give them life.

O LOVE most wise, what a sweet medicament thou dost prepare, that universal ruin may be averted! Oh what a healing remedy thou dost apply, that thou mayest cure the wound of our race! o LOVE, thy counsel is the help of the hopeless. Thou dost condemn Him who is blameless, that thou mayest save wretches who are guilty. Thou dost shed innocent blood, that thou mayest appease the wrath of Justice and draw down the clemency of the Father upon the poor and needy. O most wise

[16] Cf. Wisd. 8:1.   [17] Cf. John 12:32.

LOVE, thy sentence is the wretch's relief. Thou dost plead the cause of peace. Thou dost hear the appeal of mercy. With thy prudent counsel thou dost relieve the anguish of mankind through the most gracious will of thy clemency. Thou dost put an end unto the misery of all men through the glorious masterpiece of thy mercy. O LOVE, the secret which thou hast discovered doth offer salvation unto all who were lost.

Now, O WISDOM, behold, the storehouse of thy kindness is open. Come, look upon me in my wretchedness, as I stand without at the gate of thy charity. Come, pour the blessing of thy sweetness into the little cloak of my poverty. See, I am holding out unto thee the little empty bowl of my desire; draw back the bolt of thy plenteous store. Teach my heart thy chaste counsels, thy luminous precepts, and thy faithful testimonies.[18] Fix thy commandments in my mind, that I may fulfil them.[19] Come, my Jesus, deal not with me according to my sins, and reward me not according to my iniquities.[20] Come, as Thou hast truly atoned for me in Thy blood, restore unto me, through the virtue of Thy precious cross, all that I have lost in the course of my life. Come, O LOVE most wise, cover and bury all my sins. Do thou atone for all my heedlessness, through my Jesus, who of His own accord delivered Himself unto thy will.

5

At the hour of None, hold converse with LOVE *and* DIVINE PREDILECTION, *that they may take pity on thy woes, and thou mayest inclose thy death in the death of the Lamb, and, under such protection, pass safely out of this world. Now therefore recite this next strophe:*

> Thou, being rich, didst become poor;
> Thou wast crucified for our sake;
> Wash us in the water which flowed from Thy side
> And cleanse us of the life of our old selves.

[18] See Ps. 18:8-9.   [19] Cf. Ps. 102:18.   [20] Cf. Ps. 102:10.

Be Thou swayed by Thy compassion and put an end unto our woes by Thy pardon! In spite of my unworthiness, hear my request and satisfy me at the hour of death with the immediate vision of Thy sweet countenance, that I may have eternal rest in Thee.

O beautiful PREDILECTION of God! O CHARITY, thou flame stronger than death! [21] For fallen creatures, thou art the atonement; of the whole world, thou art the salvation and the redemption. How pleasant are thy words, and how lovely thy conversation! Thy society hath no tediousness, and thy company is true and endless joy.[22] Come, enter my poor dwelling and rest with me. Thou tellest of the Holy Spirit; let me hear thy colloquies, that with thee I may forget all my anguish and my tribulations. In this path wherein I walk, be thou with me, for all blessings come unto me together with thee.

O august PREDILECTION, behold, I am tossed about by the strong wind of my heedlessness, and my conscience is terrified by the thunder of my sins. Poor little waif that I am, I would fain take refuge beneath the roof of thy compassion, for my last hope do I place in thee, and my rest do I find only in thee. Thou, like a mother, dost cherish me, thy lost child, in thy bosom. Thou, in thy most provident and considered counsel, dost abuse the Son of the Most High, nor dost thou spare Him even death itself, that thou mayest succor man in his despair.

O CHARITY, O PREDILECTION, thou for poor sinners hast so used the Son of the Virgin, that unto all the despairing thou hast given hope in thee. Thou by thy kindness dost constrain all men to trust in thee; and that no wretch may plead against thee, thou dost champion the cause of all, to their salvation. O CHARITY, do thou prepare for me in thee a council chamber, a nest where, beggared and forsaken as I am, I may find refuge and rest for my troubled spirit. Do thou endure with me the strife of my earthly sojourning. Do thou rouse the timidity of

21 See Cant. 8:6. 22 See Wisd. 8:16.

my spirit. Do thou comfort the anguish of my heart and say unto me: "I will not forget thee!" Come, O CHARITY, honor the word thou hast spoken and deign to invite me unto thy festivals, for my soul longeth ardently for thy market days, that in thy sacred barter thou mayest take my woes and grant me in exchange thy blessings. Thou dost hold my Jesus, my sweet Saviour, so firmly fixed unto the cross, that fainting beneath thy hand He hath died of love.

O CHARITY, what dost thou? Unto whom goest thou? Thou wilt spare naught, thou wilt not rest, until thou hast succored the wretched. Thou settest no bounds unto love. Thou dost so afflict with thirst Him who is the Fount of life, that one death doth not suffice Him; but dying He giveth Himself unto love anew, and yearneth and thirsteth to die a fresh death for each single soul, redeeming the lost at a dearer price. O LOVE, thy devising hath touched the sinew of my Jesus' Heart so shrewdly, that because of love it hath shrunk and been brought to naught.[23] O LOVE, now have enough, now set thyself some bounds, since my Jesus hangeth dead before thy eyes! He is dead, He is proven to be dead, that I may have life more abundantly.[24] He is dead, that the Father might adopt me as His child more tenderly; He is dead, that I might live more happily.

O dearest death of Christ, thou art my happiest possession. I beg thee, let my soul find a nest for itself in thee, O death! O death, thou bringest forth the fruits of eternal life. Let the life-giving floods that flow from thee, I beg thee, overwhelm me. O death, thou art eternal life; I beg thee, let me ever hope beneath thy wings.[25] O wholesome death, let my soul, I beg thee, dwell amid thy glorious blessings. O most precious death, thou art the dearest thing I own. I beg thee, engulf my whole life in thyself and immerse my death in thee.

O most efficacious death of Christ, let my death, I pray thee, be safe and tranquil under thy protection. O life-giving death,

[23] See Gen. 32:24-25.   [24] Cf. John 10:10.   [25] Cf. Ps. 90:4.

let me melt away beneath thy wings. O death whence floweth life, let one treasured spark of that life coming from thee burn within me for evermore. O glorious death! O fruitful death! O death, the sum of all my salvation, thou art the beloved covenant of my redemption, the firm pact of my reconciliation! O triumphant, sweet, and life-giving death, in thee shineth forth such great charity towards me that its like is not found in heaven or on earth.

O most heartfelt death of Christ, thou art the source of my heart's confidence. O most loving death, all blessings are stored up for me in thee. Come, be my guardian, that when I die I may rest softly beneath thy shadow. O most merciful death, thou art my most happy life. Thou art my most plenteous redemption. Thou art my most glorious inheritance. Come, infold me utterly in thee, hide my whole life in thee, bury my death in thee.

O most consoling death of Christ, do thou make preparation for my death; shelter me about when the anguish of death cometh. Through thee may I have a safe passage, a death unmolested by robbers. In the lap of thy most precious redemption, take up my spirit. On the couch of thy most abundant charity, receive my soul. In thee, engulf my life; in thee, immerse me utterly. O dearest death, in thee make ready then for me a place of rest. Let me in thee happily breathe my last and sweetly fall asleep. O most heartfelt death, do thou keep me now for ever thine, in thy fatherly charity, to belong unto thee as thy everlasting possession.

O LOVE, thou didst win for me that most wholesome death of Christ, that dearest of my possessions. Thou hast dealt so wondrously with me, that thou hast bound me eternally unto thy service. What shall I give back unto thee for such infinite blessings? [26] What praise or thanksgiving can I offer thee, though I try a thousand times over? What am I, a poor little

26 Cf. Ps. 115:12.

creature, compared with Thee, O my plentiful Redemption? I will offer Thee therefore my whole soul, which Thou hast redeemed, and I will confer upon Thee the love of my heart. Come, do Thou transform my life in Thee. Receive my whole self in Thee; inclose me in Thee and make me one with Thee.

O Divine LOVE, thy ardor hath thrown open unto me the beloved Heart of my Jesus. O Heart, fountain of sweetness! O Heart surging with compassion! O Heart overflowing with charity! O Heart distilling tenderness! O Heart full of mercy! Come, let me die of love and affection for Thee. O dearest Heart, I pray Thee, engulf my whole heart in Thee. O my heart's dearest treasure, do Thou invite me unto Thy life-giving banquet. Give me to drink, unworthy as I am, of the wine of Thy comfort; in Thy Divine charity raise up the ruins of my spirit, and out of Thy superabundance of charity atone for all the beggary and neediness of my soul.

O LOVE, I pray thee now to offer for me, before the golden altar of man's reconciliation, this Heart, this most fragrant perfume, this sweetest incense, this most worthy sacrifice, in atonement for all the days I have lived wherein I have brought forth unto thee no fruit. O LOVE, in the flood tide of this glorious Heart immerse my spirit, and in the abyss of the Divine mercy bury all the load of my iniquity and heedlessness. Restore unto me in Jesus an understanding most clear and affections most pure. Disengage my heart from all fleshliness and set it free from alien love, that at the hour of my death, under thy leading, I may present it unto God immaculate.

O Heart exceedingly beloved, unto Thee my heart now crieth! Be Thou mindful of me; let the sweetness of Thy charity, I beseech Thee, refresh my heart. Come, let the depths of Thy mercy be moved with pity for me, for, alas! my ill deeds are many, and of merits I have none. O my Jesus, grant that the merits of Thy precious death (which alone suffice to pay the debt of all mankind) may forgive me in Thee whatever ill I have deserved and give me back in Thee all the blessings which I have lost. Let me thus be so powerfully converted unto Thee, that being utterly transformed by the ardor of Divine love, I may find in Thy eyes that favor and obtain that mercy which Thou didst merit for me when, for love of my love, Thou didst die upon the cross. And grant, O dearest Jesus, that I may love Thee in all things and above all things, cleave unto Thee fervently, and hope in Thee with boundless trust.

Grant me, in fine, so to pay homage unto Thy death, that in the hour of my death, free from tarrying, I may deserve to experience the sweetest fruit of my redemption and the incomparable merits of Thy death, with as great efficacy as Thou didst desire for me, when, athirst for my salvation, Thou didst breathe forth Thy spirit and didst redeem me at the great price of Thy precious blood. O LOVE, at my death bid me a sweet farewell, that in thee I may sweetly rest in peace. Amen.

6

At the hour of Vespers, in thy endeavor to appease God, thou shalt seek the company of LOVE *and* COMPASSION, *that at the end of thy life they may answer for thee unto the Lord regarding all thy debts and imperfections. Now therefore recite this next strophe:*

> Happy is CHARITY who thirsteth for Thee,
> O Truth, who art the fountain of life!
> Most blessed is that throng
> Whose eyes contemplate Thee.

Be Thou swayed by Thy compassion and put an end unto our woes by Thy pardon! In spite of my unworthiness, hear my request and satisfy me at the hour of death with the immediate vision of Thy sweet countenance, that I may have eternal rest in Thee.

O lovely COMPASSION of God! O dear liberality of God! Thou dost open thy arms unto all men; thou art the refuge of the poor. O COMPASSION, what dost thou counsel? Whither shall I fly to escape from the cold, for I cannot bear the severity of winter? The lukewarmness of my soul hath already chilled with frost the fields of my heart. Come, overshadow me with thy shoulders; hide me, lest my nakedness put me to shame. Let me warm myself beneath thy pinions, and hope for evermore beneath thy wings.[27]

O COMPASSION, COMPASSION, forsake me not in my anguish! Turn not away thy face from my sobs and my cries. Be thou swayed by thy charity and hear me with patience. Come, hold out unto me thy arms and let me rest for a little upon thy breast and pour out my soul unto thee. I put my trust in thy goodness and in thy innate compassion; for thou spurnest not one who is desolate; thou despisest not one who is troubled. How affable and kind art thou unto the wretched, and how welcome is the fragrance of thy perfumes unto the faint of spirit!

Thou dost raise up the fallen; thou dost loose prisoners from their chains.[28] Thou despisest not him who is in tribulation; thou turnest thy motherly gaze with mercy upon all who are destitute. Most kindly dost thou counsel the desperate; with clemency dost thou succor all who are in want. Now lend an ear unto me in my need and grant me what thou dost accord so seldom, a tryst for my soul with thee, that I may receive thy precious counsels.

Behold, at the thought of my sins I begin to be seized with alarm; for all the good deeds I have left undone, I blush with shame; because I have ruined my life, I tremble with fright. I fear that examination which is to come, when, like unto the nobleman in the parable,[29] Christ will hold a reckoning with me. Should He demand that I restore those moneys of time which He gave me in trust, and the interest upon the talent of understanding which He confided unto me, to satisfy His charity I shall find no answer.

[27] Cf. Ps. 90:4.   [28] Cf. Ps. 145:7-8.   [29] See Luke 19:12.

What shall I do? Whither shall I turn? To dig, I have not strength; to become a beggar, I am ashamed.[30] O COMPASSION, be thou not silent now; I beseech thee, let thy gentle counsel revive my spirit. Come, answer me; tell me what thou deemest best for me in these straits; for according to thy name, thou art in truth compassionate of heart and knowest best what will avail me now. Come, have mercy upon me and succor me, and be not thou unfavorable unto me in this distress of mine. Let the poverty of my spirit move thee; let thy heart be touched with pity, and say thou unto me compassionately: "Thou and I shall have but one purse between us!"[31]

O COMPASSION, thou hast dazzling riches laid up in such abundance that heaven and earth together cannot hold them. Thou didst constrain my Jesus to give His soul for my soul, His life for my life, that thou mightest make mine all that is His, and thus, out of thy affluence, the beggar's store might be increased. I beseech thee, call my famished soul unto thy table, that I may live upon thy riches. Cherish me, nourish me, that I may not faint in the service of the Lord, until under thy guidance I return unto God and yield up my spirit unto Him who gave it.[32]

O COMPASSION, O bounty, O dear liberality of God, thou dost guard in thy treasure house a most wondrous gift, whereat heaven is amazed and earth doth marvel, the like whereof hath never yet been found nor ever shall be. Every day at the altar thou offerest for me unto God the Father a sacrifice, a burnt offering, an incense which surpasseth all deserving and in truth availeth to cancel all my debts. Thou offerest unto the Father that Son in whom He is truly well pleased, that thou mayest truly appease Him towards me and reconcile me unto Him.

Come, by this sacrament which can best make amends for my imperfections and atone for all my failures, do thou renew my life and restore unto me a hundredfold all that I have lost.

30 *Ibid.* 16:3.   31 Cf. Prov. 1:14.   32 Cf. Eccles. 12:7.

Then my soul will rejoice in thee, my youth will be renewed like the eagle's [33] through thee, all my life will be transformed by thy influence, all my strength will serve thee, and all my being will glorify thee. O my Jesus, by Thy compassion blot out all my iniquities; by Thy charity, cover and bury all my sins; by Thy predilection, atone for all my heedlessness; by Thy love, re-establish me in that liberty of spirit wherewith Thou, who art innocence itself, dying for me, at the price of Thy own blood didst set me free. Make me conform unto Thy will, that I may transform my life in Thee. Make me wholly and entirely what Thou wouldst have me be, that after this life, emerging from the cloud of my flesh, I may come with jubilation unto the vision of Thy glorious face.

7

At the hour of Compline, hold converse with LOVE *and* PERSEVERANCE, *that thou mayest exchange thy wretched life with the most venerable life of Jesus, and through Him mayest be found, at the hour of thy death, replete with sanctity and the full perfection of the monastic state. Now therefore recite this final strophe:*

> Great is the glory given unto Thee
> By the memory of Thy praise,
> Which they who lift up their hearts out of the depths
> Do celebrate without ceasing.

Be Thou swayed by Thy compassion and put an end unto our woes by Thy pardon! In spite of my unworthiness, hear my request and satisfy me at the hour of death with the immediate vision of Thy sweet countenance, that I may have eternal rest in Thee.

O persevering CHARITY of the Lord Jesus who hath loved us unto death, thou alone wearest the regal diadem. To thee be-

[33] Cf. Ps. 102:5.

longeth the triumph of the victory and the title of glory. Thy far sighted labor, thy watch and ward, have brought unto the King of Kings gifts of such splendor that heaven looketh on amazed.

O persevering CHARITY, in truth thy voice is sweet and sonorous; thy face is gentle and beautiful. Thou gatherest even in the desert such rare gifts and the perfume of such varied virtues, that the God of heaven honoreth thy face with His favor, praising and desiring thy comeliness and beauty.[34] Thee hath God chosen, to look upon thee and to help thee; for He who is immutable reposeth in thee as the Bridegroom in His nuptial chamber. Succor me in the morning early;[35] O thou who art the true noontide, preserve my soul in thyself from the blindness that cometh at twilight.

O persevering CHARITY, thou art the perfection of all virtues; thou art the health of my spirit. Thou makest heavy burdens grow light; from thy usage all the virtues come to be familiar, and the labors which they exact become pleasant. O perfect Charity of God, in thee are all sweetness and delight. Thou art true peace and security. In thee are peace and tranquillity that cannot be disturbed. Thou art the end and perfection of all good deeds, the fulfilment of the commandments of God. Thou art the sabbath of sabbaths. In thee, Wisdom findeth His repose; in thee, Love perfecteth His work.

O persevering CHARITY, thou didst consummate in my Jesus the work which compassion laid upon Him. Thou didst accomplish the work of our redemption, that thou mightest bring back them who were lost into the state of adoption. Thou makest my Jesus fall gently asleep in peace; thou makest Him rest in thee after His labor and recline under thy shade; thou makest Him keep the repose of the sabbath and, enclosed and entombed under thy seal, take His slumber of love.

O CHARITY, keep watch and ward with thy utmost vigilance

34 See Ps. 44:12, 5.   35 Cf. Ps. 45:6.

over Him who is the inestimable price of my soul, over Him who is more desirable than gold or topaz;[36] He alone can retrieve all my failures and redress all my imperfections. Thou hast laid away within thee my dearest treasure; come, lay away my heart there also, that thanks unto thee my whole spirit may abide where my dearest Beloved dwelleth.

O CHARITY, thou who art life, O strong PERSEVERANCE of the Lord Jesus, unto thee out of the depths of my heart mounteth the cry of my spirit! Come, be thou my ambassador and speak in my favor. Through thee my Jesus, my King and my God, brought to completion the work which the Father had given Him to accomplish. Through thee likewise, despite my worthlessness, may He give me a pure heart; an invincible spirit wherewith to serve Him in all diligence, fidelity, and zeal; and perseverance in bearing His commandments, with my shoulders willingly bowed beneath the yoke of His love. Then, O efficacious LOVE, both in my life and after my death, thou thyself shalt be my true recompense a hundredfold,[37] and I shall receive thee as my crown, for in thee is the sum of all my joy.

Give me loving contrition and humble repentance, whereby to take the place which I have deserved by my sins; not amongst the children of the kingdom, but amongst the dogs. Then after this life, like the woman of Canaan, I shall receive the most blessed crumbs fallen from the children's table;[38] I mean, the most blessed fruition of the glorious face of my Jesus, that through thee I may be satisfied in eternal happiness, when the glory of my Jesus appeareth.[39]

O LOVE who art steadfast, strong, and unconquerable, teach me by thy rare skill to love Jesus with invincible constancy and serve Him with weariless perseverance. Arouse me and urge me to keep myself ever ready for the coming of my Lord in the first or the second watch,[40] that being neither inert nor sunken

---

[36] Cf. Ps. 118:127. [37] See Matt. 19:29. [38] See *ibid.* 15:27.
[39] Cf. Ps. 16:15. [40] See Luke 12:38.

in slumber when the midnight cry resoundeth, I may be worthy, at thy bidding and under thy guidance, to go in with the Lamb unto the marriage. In that hour, let my lamp, thanks to thy providing, be found full of the oil of charity, full of the fire of love,[41] full of the dazzling light of the works of living faith, that through thee I may possess the delights of eternal life.

Now, my dearest Jesus, Bridegroom beloved, grant resurrection in Thee unto my sluggish spirit; by Thy death restore unto me a life which liveth for Thee alone. Grant that my way of life may be worthy of the price of Thy blood. Give me a spirit which tasteth Thee, thoughts which think of Thee, a soul which understandeth Thy will, strength which accomplisheth Thy good pleasure, and stability which persevereth with Thee. Come, and at the hour of my death open unto me without delay the door of Thy most benign Heart, that through Thee I may deserve to enter unhindered into the bridechamber of Thy living love, where I shall enjoy and possess Thee, O Thou true joy of my heart! Amen.

II

At noontide on the day when thou dost solemnize this atonement, pray unto the Lord to admit thee into the pleasure garden of His Divine Heart, that thou mayest there be washed seven times in the Jordan[42] of the merits of His life and passion. Thus on the day of thy death thou wilt be all fair,[43] having been purified from every stain, and wilt find thyself admitted into the bridechamber of His Divine love.

1

O Jesus, my Life and my Saviour, Thou comest in all the splendor of Thy beauty from the land of the angels; but my soul, Thy beloved creature, dwelleth, alas! in the gloom of blindness. Come, be Thou my salvation and my perfect light.

---

[41] See Matt. 25:4-6.   [42] See 4 Kgs. 5:10.   [43] Cant. 4:7.

O my Beloved, by the pure tears of Thy lucent eyes, wash away all the stains of the sins of my eyes, that at the end of my life, with the pure eyes of my heart, I may without hindrance behold in the mirror of the Holy Trinity Thy adorable face, for Thou alone art He whom my whole heart desireth. Come swiftly and immerse me in the abyss of fruition of Thee.

2

O Jesus, my blissful hope, Bridegroom most faithful and most merciful, Thou who dost never scorn the sighs of the wretched, by my own fault my ear, alas! hath become deaf. Come, O Father of mercies,[44] let me obey Thee with a docile ear my whole life long. O my Beloved, by the sweet compassion of Thy blessed ears, wash away all the wickedness of the sins of my ears, that when Thou callest me at the hour of my death, I may not fear the hearing of condemnation, but hearken unto Thy voice with joy and gladness, because Thou alone art He for whom I long. Come, take me up swiftly unto Thy nuptials.

3

O eternal sweetness of my soul, Thou who alone art the Beloved of my heart, Thy face is all lovely and Thy Heart all inviting; but my thoughts, alas! go wandering far from Thee. Come, O God of my heart, gather together my scattered mental powers and fix them upon Thyself. O my Beloved, by the pure intention of Thy most holy thoughts and the ardent love of Thy transpierced Heart, wash away all the guilt of my evil thoughts and of my sinful heart, that Thy most bitter passion may be my shady bower in death, and Thy Heart, broken by love, my everlasting dwelling place, because Thou alone art He whom I have chosen rather than all created things. Come, suffer

44 2 Cor. 1:3.

me not to keep aloof for a long time from Thee, O sole Beloved of my heart!

4

O Jesus, Thou only-Begotten of the heavenly Father, O compassionate and merciful Lord, Thou who dost never leave the
children of Thy adoption in desolation, with my tongue, alas!
I have fallen into many sins. O Thou who art my glory,[45] come,
fill my mouth with Thy praise.[46] O my Beloved, by the living
power of the gentle words of Thy blessed mouth, wipe away
all the offences of my unclean mouth, that in the kiss of Thy
beatific peace I may joyfully pass from this world, for only Thy
glorious mouth can give solace unto my inmost heart. Come,
O beautiful Love, transpierce my heart with the dart of Thy
living predilection, that dying I may fall into the abyss of life
whereof Thou art the source.

5

O Jesus, Thou all-wise workman, Thou incomparable master
craftsman, Thou who hast so marvellously repaired the work
of Thy hands which I destroyed, all my works, alas! are im-
perfect and not according to Thy law. O Thou who art my
refuge and my strength, come, let every work of mine be sanctified by the cooperation of Thy living love. O my Beloved, by
the perfection of Thy works and the crucifixion of Thy hands,
wash away all the misdeeds of my impious hands, that in the
hour of my death I may cast myself without hindrance or delay
into Thy Divine embrace, for Thou art the Bridegroom of my
troth, chosen from among thousands.[47] Come, in my last hour,
through no merits of mine but out of Thy Divine bounty, acknowledge me to be Thy own.

6

O Jesus, Thou youth all-lovely, all-amiable, and all-desirable,

[45] Ps. 3:4.   [46] Cf. Ps. 70:8.   [47] Cant. 5:10.

how enrapturing Thy Divine companionship! But I, alas! have strayed from the path of righteousness and have not kept Thy commandments. Come, guide me lovingly and direct my steps according to Thy will. O my Beloved, by the painful weariness and by the piercing inflicted, through God's plan, upon Thy blessed feet, wash away all the stains of the sins of my feet, that thanks unto Thee, O faithful escort of my wayfaring, I may joyfully cross the threshold of the wondrous tabernacle and enter the house of God,[48] because Thou art the crown for whose sake I am running my course.[49] Come, grant me an impetuous love to rouse me from my lassitude and heedlessness and urge me to run ever onward after Thee.

7

O Jesus, Thou God of might, who art most kind and most liberal, Thy gifts are never niggardly! O Thou living God, the inflow of Thy burning love draweth back into Thy bosom all beings which have ever flowed forth from Thee; but all my life, alas! is lost, withered, and brought to naught. Come, O God of my life, let my life grow green again in Thee, put forth new flowers, and regain the strength to bear its due fruit. O my Beloved, by the exalted innocence and flawless sanctity of Thy life, wash away all the foulness of my corrupt life, that my life may no longer be with me, but by the force of Thy burning love may be wholly transported into Thee. Then in the hour of my death I shall rejoice, O my true Life! to find myself in Thee, for Thou art my supreme and dearest Good, Thou alone art the refuge of my soul. Come, grant that I may grow faint with love for Thee, die of desire for Thee, praise Thee with jubilation, and be for all eternity enkindled with the blazing fire of Thy charity. Amen.

[48] Ps. 41:5.   [49] Cf. 1 Cor. 9:24.

III

At eventide, as if thou wert gathering flowers in company with thy Beloved, pray that He may grant thee His blessing and the virtues which thou dost desire.

This day, O dearest Jesus, I beseech Thee, may Thy soul bless me. May Thy ever-reigning Godhead bless me. May Thy fruitful Manhood bless me most powerfully, and Thy regal munificence leave me such unmistakable tokens of Thy blessing, that by invincible love I may be wholly transformed from myself into Thee and cleave unto Thee in deathless union. Make me perfect in Thy love. Make me pleasing unto Thee in humility of spirit, in fraternal charity, in chaste simplicity, in humble reverence, in purity of heart, in watchfulness over my senses, in holiness of life, in prompt obedience, in gentle patience, in spiritual knowledge, in freely chosen poverty, in holy mildness, in gravity of manners, in cheerfulness of spirit, in all truth, in a good conscience, in constancy of faith, in holy perseverance, in the strength of hope, in the fulness of charity, and in the blessed perfection of Thy love; that the thorny thicket of my heart may be changed into a paradise of all the virtues and an arbor of all perfection, like a field which the Lord hath blessed,[50] full of peace, sanctity, and filial love of God.

Come, most dearly beloved Jesus, be Thou always with me, that my heart may abide with Thee and Thy love persevere immovably with me; then my death shall be so blessed by Thee that my spirit, having cast off the bonds of the flesh, will straightway rest in Thee. Amen.

[50] Cf. Gen. 27:27.

List of Liturgical Texts

SECOND EXERCISE

Come, Holy Spirit.

Veni, sancte Spiritus, reple tuorum corda fidelium: et tui amoris in eis ignem accende.

Saint Gertrude has freely paraphrased this familiar text from the Mass of Pentecost.

RESPONSORY. The kingdom of the world.

VERSE. My heart hath uttered.

R. Regnum mundi et omnem ornatum saeculi contempsi propter amorem Domini mei Jesu Christi, * Quem vidi, quem amavi, in quem credidi, quem dilexi. V. Eructavit cor meum verbum bonum, dico ego opera mea regi.

This responsory is found in the third and fourth Exercises; it also appears several times in the *Herald of Divine Love,* as well as in the *Book of Special Grace* and *The Flowing Light of the Godhead.* See *Revelationes Gertrudianae ac Mechtildianiae,* I (Paris, 1875), *Legatus Divinae Pietatis,* Lib. IV, cap. 54, pp. 467 ff., Lib. V, cap. 1, p. 515; and II (Paris, 1877), *Liber Specialis Gratiae,* Pars VII, cap. 18, pp. 413-414. *The Revelations of Mechthild of Magdeburg (1210-1297) or The Flowing Light of the Godhead,* translated by Lucy Menzies (London,

1953), Part VIII. 10, p. 217. At Helfta it was sung at the nuns' funerals and in times of special need.

RESPONSORY. O Christ, true author.

VERSE. Thou art the fount.

> R. Verae pudicitiae auctor et custos virginitatis qui ex Virgine natus multos excitasti ad sanctum amorem castitatis animos; * Qui es perpes corona virginum, per merita earum nos adjuva. V. Fons vitae et origo totius bonitatis, duc nos ad portum salutis.

In the *Herald,* this text is referred to in the chapter on the feast of the eleven thousand virgins, October 21st. See *Legatus,* Lib. IV, cap. 54, p. 468.

THIRD EXERCISE

ANTIPHON. Come ye! Come ye! Come ye!

> Venite, venite, venite, filiae, audite me, timorem Domini docebo vos.

The rite of invitation is found in a more complete form in the fourth Exercise. It is not, in fact, confined to the ceremony of consecration, and occurs notably in the reconciliation of penitents assigned in the Pontifical to Holy Thursday. See René Metz, *La consécration des vierges dans l'Eglise romaine, étude d'histoire de la liturgie* (Paris, 1954), pp. 283-285; p. 321, note 13; pp. 330-331; pp. 350-351. *Pontificale Romanum* (Mechlin, 1934), De reconciliatione poenitentium, pp. 730 ff. Dom André Mocquereau, *Paléographie musicale,* XII (Tournay, 1922), plate 211.

ANTIPHON. I come.

> Et nunc sequimur in toto corde; timemus te, et quaerimus faciem tuam videre; Domine, ne confundas nos, sed fac nobis juxta mansuetudinem tuam, et secundum multitudinem misericordiae tuae.

The source of this text is Daniel 3:41-42. Like all the other texts in the third Exercise (except the three which will be pointed out), it is found in the ceremony of consecration.

VERSE. Receive me.

> Suscipe me, Domine, secundum eloquium tuum, et vivam. Et non confundas me ab exspectatione mea.

The source of this text is Psalm 118:116. Its place in the Benedictine profession ceremony is explained in the commentary on the fourth Exercise.

PRAYER. O God, who in Thy gracious kindness.

> Deus, castorum corporum, etc. This long prayer of consecration, which is sung by the bishop in the form of a preface, is found in the *Pontificale Romanum,* pp. 271 ff. Its history is fully set forth by Metz, *La consécration des vierges*; see p. 202, note 136.

RESPONSORY. The Lord hath clad me.

VERSE. The Lord hath clad me.

> R. Induit me Dominus vestimento salutis, et indumento laetitiae circumdedit me; * Et tamquam sponsam decoravit me corona.

This responsory is mentioned in the *Herald* among other liturgical texts, concerning which Saint Gertrude received special illuminations. See *Legatus,* Lib. III, cap. 30, p. 183.

The "verse" given by her in the present Exercise, "The Lord hath clad me with a dress woven of gold," does not belong to this responsory, but is really an antiphon. The Latin text is as follows:

> Induit me Dominus cyclade auro texta, et immensis monilibus ornavit me.

M. Metz' exhaustive study of the ceremony of consecration nowhere mentions this responsory, or the two which follow in the third Exercise; but the verses are the same texts as three antiphons which are sung during the ceremony by the chosen nuns. Like the other antiphons (and the responsories) in the third Exercise, they are taken from the office of Saint Agnes, January 21st.

ANTIPHON. He hath put a mark.

> Posuit signum in faciem meam, ut nullum praeter eum amatorem admittam.

RESPONSORY. Christ do I love.

VERSE. Honey and milk.

> R. Amo Christum, in cujus thalamum introibo, cujus mater virgo est, cujus pater feminam nescit, cujus mihi organa modulatis vocibus cantant: * Quem cum amavero, casta sum; cum tetigero, munda sum; cum accepero, virgo sum. V. Mel et lac ex ejus ore suscepi, et sanguis ejus ornavit genas meas.

This responsory is alluded to in the *Book of Special Grace,* in the account of visions seen by Saint Mechtild on the feast of Saint Agnes. See *Liber Specialis Gratiae,* Pars I, cap. 11, p. 34.

In the modern Monastic Breviary, the verse "Mel et lac" does not appear in this responsory; but it is found as Saint Gertrude gives it, in the thirteenth century antiphonal reproduced by the monks of Solesmes in *Paléographie Musicale,* Vol. XII, plate 254.

ANTIPHON. His ring.

> Anulo suo subarrhavit me Dominus meus Jesus Christus, et tamquam sponsam decoravit me corona.

In the present Exercise, Saint Gertrude has altered this antiphon. She quotes it literally, however, in the short chapter entitled: "The rings of spiritual espousals" in the *Herald.* See *Legatus,* Lib. III, cap. 2, p. 120. Here she relates that our Lord once appeared to her, bearing two gold rings, set with jewels, which symbolized delight and suffering. She "understood that as the ring is the sign of espousals, so adversity, whether bodily or spiritual, is the indubitable sign of the Divine choice and, as it were, the espousals of the soul with God. For this reason anyone who suffers may say confidently and in all truth, 'His ring my Lord Jesus Christ hath given me in pledge.' And if in the midst of her trouble the soul does not lack the gift of being able to turn to God in gratitude, with praise and thanksgiving, she may joyfully add this also: 'And He hath adorned me like a bride with a crown.' For gratitude amid trouble is a most brilliant crown, far more precious than gold or topaz."

RESPONSORY. His Body.

VERSE. I am wedded.

> R. Jam corpus ejus corpori meo sociatum est, et sanguis ejus ornavit genas meas: * Cujus mater virgo est, cujus pater feminam nescit. V. Ipsi sum desponsata, cui Angeli serviunt, cujus pulchritudinem sol et luna mirantur.

In the *Herald,* Saint Gertrude tells us that one day as she stood in the cloister at noon, the brilliance of the sun reminded her of this verse. See *Legatus,* Lib. II, cap. 17, p. 90.

PRAYER. Grant, I beseech Thee.

> Da, quaesumus, omnipotens Deus, ut haec famula tua, quae pro spe retributionis aeternae, tibi Domino desiderat consecrari, plena fide animoque in sancto proposito permaneat. Tu eam omnipotens Pater sanctificare et benedicere, et in perpetuum conservare, digneris. Tribue ei humilitatem, castitatem, obedientiam, charitatem, et omnium bonorum operum quantitatem: da ei Domine pro operibus gloriam, pro pudore reverentiam, pro pudicitia sanctitatem, ut ad meritum possit gloriae pervenire.

Saint Gertrude knew the text of this prayer as it appears in the Pontifical of Mainz, dating from the middle of the tenth century (see Metz, *La consécration des vierges,* p. 204, note 150), and not in the short form of the modern Pontifical (see *Pontificale Romanum,* p. 288).

May the Divine majesty.

> Benedicat vos Conditor coeli et terrae, Deus Pater omnipotens, qui vos eligere dignatus est ad beatae Mariae matris Domini nostri Jesu Christi consortium; ut integram et immaculatam virginitatem quam professae estis, coram Deo et angelis ejus conservetis; propositum teneatis; castitatem diligatis; patientiam custodiatis; ut coronam virginitatis accipere mereamini.

See *Pontificale Romanum,* p. 287; Metz, *La consécration des vierges,* p. 306, note 112.

HYMN. Thee, O God, do we praise.

> Te Deum laudamus, etc.

This familiar text needs no comment.

FOURTH EXERCISE

And behold I come.

> Et ecce venio ad te quem amavi, in quem credidi, quem dilexi.

This may be the text alluded to by Metz, *La consécration des vierges,* p. 236, note 57.

PRAYER. O Jesus, Thou good Shepherd.

> . . . Praesta ut haec vox invitationis tuae ita in eo convalescat, quatenus peccatorum onera deponens, et quam dulcis es gustans, tua refectione sustentari mereatur. Et sicut attestari de ovibus tuis dignatus es, agnosce eum inter oves tuas: ut ipse te agnoscat, et alienum non sequatur, sed te; neque audiat vocem aliorum, sed tuam, qua dicis: Qui mihi ministrat, me sequatur.

This text is the last part of the third *oratio* for the profession of monks. See *Pontificale Romanum,* De benedictione abbatis, p. 204.

ANTIPHON. Draw near unto Him.

> Accedite ad eum et illuminamini, et facies vestrae non confundentur.

This antiphon, together with Psalm 33, is found immediately following the triple repetition of the antiphon *Venite* in the rite for the reconciliation of penitents, *Pontificale Romanum,* p. 731.

ANTIPHON. This is the generation.

> Haec est generatio quaerentium Dominum, quaerentium faciem Dei Jacob.

This antiphon, together with Psalm 23, is found in the common of martyrs in the thirteenth century antiphonal. See *Paléographie musicale,* XII, plate 421.

ANTIPHON. Create a clean heart.

> Cor mundum crea in me Deus, et spiritum rectum innova in visceribus meis.

In the rite for the reconciliation of penitents already mentioned, this antiphon is found together with Psalm 50. See *Pontificale Romanum,* p. 740; *Paléographie musicale,* XII, plate 211 (also plates 88 and 206).

ANTIPHON. He that dwelleth.

> Qui habitat in adjutorio Altissimi, in protectione Dei coeli commorabitur.

This antiphon and psalm are found in the office of the dedication of a church.

RESPONSORY. Send forth Wisdom.

VERSE. Give unto me Wisdom.

> R. Emitte, Domine, Sapientiam de sede magnitudinis tuae,

ut mecum sit et mecum laboret: * Ut sciam quid accep-
tum sit coram te omni tempore. V. Da mihi, Domine,
sedium tuarum assistricem sapientiam.

This is a responsory appointed for the month of August. It
is quoted in the *Book of Special Grace* as the prayer which
should be offered by anyone who is in trouble, in humble sub-
mission to God's designs for him. See *Liber Specialis Gratiae*,
Pars IV, cap. 25, p. 282.

RESPONSORY. I will love Thee.

VERSE. I will praise the Lord.

R. Diligam te Domine virtus mea; Dominus firmamentum
meum et refugium meum. V. Laudans invocabo Dominum
et ab inimicis meis salvus ero.

In the thirteenth century antiphonal, this is the fifth responsory for the first Sunday after Epiphany. See *Paléographie musicale*, XII, plate 61.

SEVENTH EXERCISE

HYMN. O Thou who dost liberally grant pardon.

Amorem sensus erige
Ad te, largitor veniae,
Ut fias clemens cordibus,
Purgatis inde sordibus.

Benigne multum, Domine,
Tu lapsum scis in homine:
Infirma est materia;
Versamur in miseria.

Causa tibi sit agnita:
Nulla mens est incognita;
Aufer a nobis omnia
Fallentis mundi somnia.

Externi huc advenimus,

> In exilio gemimus:
> Tu portus es et patria,
> Duc nos ad vitae atria.
>
> Dives pauper effectus es,
> Pro nobis crucifixus es;
> Lavans e tuo latere
> Nos munda vita vetere.
>
> Felix, quae sitit Charitas
> Te fontem vitae, Veritas:
> Beati valde oculi
> Te speculantis populi.
>
> Grandis est tibi gloria,
> Tuae laudis memoria,
> Quam sine fine celebrant,
> Qui cor ab imis elevant.

This hymn is found in the medieval German breviaries. See *Les Exercices de Sainte Gertrude,* translated by Dom Albert Schmitt, O.S.B. (Paris, 1942), p. 197, note 2.

HYMN. Be Thou swayed by Thy compassion.

> Tua te cogat pietas
> Ut mala nostra superes
> Parcendo, et voti compotes
> Nos tuo vultu saties.

In the *Herald,* this strophe is given as the third of a hymn beginning *Desiderate millies.* See *Legatus,* Lib. V. cap. 30, p. 602.

Notes

INTRODUCTION

1 *Revelationes Gertrudianae ac Mechtildianae, I, Sanctae Gertrudis Magnae Legatus Divinae Pietatis* (Paris, 1875), Praefatio, pp. viii-ix. This is the critical edition prepared by Dom Paquelin of Solesmes from the Vienne manuscript dated 1490. (It will be referred to as *Legatus*.) Gabriel Ledos, *Sainte Gertrude* (5th edition, Paris, 1903), p. 12.

2 *Legatus*, Praefatio, p. viii; Lib. II, cap. 3, pp. 62-63. *Le héraut de l'amour divin, Révélations de Sainte Gertrude* (new edition, Paris, 1952), I, Préface, p. x. This is the French translation of the *Legatus* made by the nuns of Our Lady of Wisques. (It will be referred to as *Le héraut.*)

3 *Le héraut*, I, Préface, pp. xi-xii. A photograph of this structure and one of the pond are reproduced in the book published under the name of Dom Gilbert Dolan, *St. Gertrude the Great* (London, 1913).

4 *Legatus*, Lib. III, cap. 18, p. 157.

5 *Ibid.*, Lib. IV, cap. 2, p. 272.

6 *Ibid.*, Lib. IV, cap. 2, p. 288; cap. 9, p. 323. *Revelationes Gertrudianae ac Mechtildianae, II, Sanctae Mechtildis Liber Specialis Gratiae* (Paris, 1877), Pars I, cap. 6, p. 21. (This will be referred to as *Liber Specialis Gratiae.*)

7 *Liber Specialis Gratiae*, Pars II, cap. 4, p. 141; cap. 19, p. 156. *Legatus*, Lib. IV, cap. 2, p. 295.

8 *Legatus*, Lib. III, cap. 31, p. 192; Lib. IV, cap. 2, p. 298. *Liber Specialis Gratiae*, Pars I, cap. 27, p. 95.

9 *Legatus*, Lib. II, cap. 2, p. 61; Lib. IV, cap. 2, pp. 293 ff.; cap. 12, pp. 333 ff.; cap. 48, pp. 432 ff. *Liber Specialis Gratiae*, Pars I, cap. 5, pp. 14-15.

10 *Legatus*, Lib. II, cap. 4, p. 66; cap. 17, p. 90.

11 *Legatus*, Praefatio, p. xxvi; Lib. II, cap. 1, p. 59. *Liber Specialis Gratiae*, Pars I, cap. 6, p. 21.

[183]

The Exercises of Saint Gertrude

12 *Legatus,* Praefatio, p. xxvi; Lib. III, cap. 28, p. 174.

13 *Ibid.,* Lib. III, cap. 69, pp. 246 ff.

14 *Ibid.,* Lib. III, cap. 32, p. 195.

15 *Legatus,* Lib. I, cap. 1, p. 7; Lib. III, cap. 28, p. 174. *Liber Specialis Gratiae,* Pars VI, cap. 1, pp. 374-375.

16 *Legatus,* Lib. III, cap. 28, p. 174. *Liber Specialis Gratiae,* Pars II, cap. 26, p. 169; Pars III, cap. 45, p. 248.

17 *Legatus,* Lib. I, cap. 1, p. 7.

18 *Liber Specialis Gratiae,* Pars VI, cap. 1, pp. 373-377.

19 *Le héraut,* I, Préface, p. xiii. Ailbe J. Luddy, O.Cist., *The Cistercian Nuns* (Dublin, 1931), pp. 16-17. Ledos, *Sainte Gertrude,* pp. 2-7.

20 *Le héraut,* I, Préface, p. xvii. Dom A. Castel, *Les belles prières de Ste Mechtilde et Ste Gertrude* (Paris, 1925), Avant-propos, pp. viii-ix.

21 Dolan, *Saint Gertrude the Great,* p. 33.

22 *Liber Specialis Gratiae,* Pars II, cap. 26, p. 169.

23 The gaps in the evidence concerning Mechtild of Magdeburg make it difficult to establish a chronology of her life. See Jeanne Ancelet-Hustache, *Mechtilde de Madgebourg (1207-1282), Etude de psychologie religieuse* (Paris, 1926), pp. 44 ff. Even if, with Mechtild's latest editor, we should accept the date of 1285 for her entrance at Helfta, the fact remains that she had been known there by reputation for some time before she was admitted; see *The Revelations of Mechthild of Magdeburg (1210-1297) or The Flowing Light of the Godhead,* translated by Lucy Menzies (London, 1953), Introduction, p. xx. It may be inferred from the *Herald* that Mechtild had even paid visits to Helfta before her entrance; see *Legatus,* Lib. I, cap. 3, p. 14, note 1.

24 *The Revelations of Mechthild of Magdeburg,* Introduction, pp. xxviii-xxix. *Cambridge Medieval History,* VII (New York, 1932), p. 800.

25 *Legatus,* Lib. V, cap. 7, pp. 542 ff. *Liber Specialis Gratiae,* Pars II, cap. 42, p. 192; Pars V, cap. 6-7, pp. 325 ff.

26 *Legatus,* Lib. II, cap. 1, pp. 59-60.

27 *Ibid.,* Lib. I, cap. 16, p. 48; Lib. II, cap. 4, p. 66.

28 *Liber Specialis Gratiae,* Pars II, cap. 42-43, pp. 190 ff.; Pars V, cap. 22, 24, 25, pp. 353 ff.; cap. 31, pp. 369-370; Pars VII, cap. 17, p. 412.

29 C. A. J. Armstrong, "The Piety of Cicely, Duchess of York," in *For Hilaire Belloc* (New York, 1942), p. 75 and p. 82.

30 *Legatus,* Lib. II, cap. 4, pp. 66 ff.; cap. 23, p. 107.

31 *Ibid.,* Lib. II, cap. 5, pp. 69 ff.; cap. 23, p. 107; Lib. V, cap. 25, p. 581. See commentary on the fifth Exercise, p. 83.

32 Dom Castel, *Les belles prières de Ste Mechtilde et de Ste Gertrude,* Avant-propos, p. xi.

NOTES

33 *The Rule of St. Benedict,* edited and translated by Abbot Justin McCann (Westminster, Maryland, 1952), Chap. 4, p. 27; Chap. 5, p. 33; etc.

34 *Legatus,* Lib. IV, cap. 25, pp. 381-383.

35 Castel, *Les belles prières de Ste Mechtilde et Ste Gertrude,* Avant-propos, pp. xi-xii.

36 *Legatus,* Lib. II, cap. 1, p. 60.

37 *The Rule of St. Benedict,* Prologue, p. 9, p. 13; Chap. 4, p. 29; etc.

38 *Legatus,* Lib. II, cap. 21, pp. 100 ff. Dom Pierre Doyère, *Le Mémorial Spirituel de Sainte Gertrude* (Paris, 1954), p. 27. Pourrat, *Christian Spirituality,* Vol. II (Westminster, Maryland, 1953), p. 90.

39 Dom Arnold Wion, O.S.B., in his book *Lignum Vitae* (Venice, 1595).

40 *Revelationes Gertrudianae ac Mechtildianae,* I, Praefatio, pp. xviii ff.

41 *Ibid.,* II, Documenta, pp. 713-714.

42 Doyère, *Le Mémorial Spirituel de Sainte Gertrude,* p. 6.

43 Alban Butler, *Lives of the Saints,* November 15. This work was first published in 1745.

44 *Legatus,* Lib. V, cap. 27, pp. 584 ff. Ledos, *Sainte Gertrude,* p. 67. Dolan, *Saint Gertrude the Great,* p. 224. We would like to think (see *Le Héraut,* II, p. 277, note 2) that this composition is nothing else than the seventh chapter of the *Exercises.* But the details given about the *Memoria Mortis,* which contained prayers appointed for five different days, seem to be irreconcilable with the text of the seventh Exercise. The latter is described in the heading as "a day of atonement," and shows no signs of a fivefold division.

45 *Legatus,* Lib. V, cap. 4, p. 523.

46 *Ibid.,* Lib. V, cap. 27, p. 586.

47 *Ibid.,* p. 590.

TRANSLATOR'S NOTE

1 Scripta Monastica, a Monachis Benedictinis Abbatiae Prataleensis Edita, N. 3 (lat.), Series Ascetico-Mystica, N. 11. *Exercitia Sanctae Gertrudis Magnae,* O.S.B., Padua, 1924.

2 *Les Exercises de Sainte Gertrude,* translated by Dom Albert Schmitt, O.S.B. (Paris, 1942), pp. 72 ff.

3 *The Book of Psalms* (Paterson, New Jersey, 1950), p. 297, note 2, 29.

4 *Revelationes Gertrudianae ac Mechtildianae,* I, Praefatio, pp. xlvi ff. Vernet, "Gertrude la Grande, Sainte," in *Dictionnaire de Theologie Catholique,* VI (Paris, 1920). Dom Oliver Kapsner, O.S.B., *A Benedictine Bibliography,* Author Part (Collegeville, 1950), pp. 148-149.

The Exercises of Saint Gertrude

COMMENTARY: FIRST EXERCISE

1 *Les Exercices de Sainte Gertrude*, translated by Dom Emmanuel, Abbot of Our Lady of Hope of the Olivetan Congregation, O.S.B. (Paris, 1919), p. 242, note 1.

COMMENTARY: SECOND EXERCISE

1 *The Rule of St. Benedict*, Chap. 58, p. 128, note 2.

2 *Legatus*, Lib. IV, cap. 28, p. 390.

3 Castel, *Les belles prières de Ste Mechtilde et de Ste Gertrude*, Avant-propos, p. viii, note 1. On the portrayal of Gertrude's habit in art, see Ancelet-Hustache, *Mechtilde de Magdebourg*, p. 60.

4 *Liber Specialis Gratiae*, Pars IV, cap. 37, p. 296.

5 *Ibid.*, Pars V, cap. 30, p. 364.

6 *Legatus*, Lib. I, cap. 11, pp. 36-37.

7 *The Rule of St. Benedict*, Prologue, p. 13.

8 *Legatus*, Lib. V, cap. 8, p. 546; see *Le heraut*, II, p. 304, note.

COMMENTARY: THIRD EXERCISE

1 René Metz, *La consécration des vierges dans l'église romaine, étude d'histoire de la liturgie* (Paris, 1954), pp. 245 ff.

2 *Revelationes Gertrudianae ac Mechtildianae*, II, Documenta, p. 716.

3 Ledos, *Sainte Gertrude*, p. 157.

4 *Legatus*, Lib. IV, cap. 29, p. 392. M. J. Ribet, *La mystique divine*, I (Paris, 1895), p. 330. *Exercitia*, p. 17.

5 *Liber Specialis Gratiae*, Pars IV, cap. 15, pp. 271-272.

6 *Ibid.*, Pars II, cap. 18, p. 153.

7 Metz, *La consécration des vierges*, p. 277.

8 *Ibid.*, p. 185, pp. 238-239. The prescriptions on this subject in the Pontifical compiled by Bishop William Durand of Mende (*ibid.*, p. 277) are of interest because this book is contemporary with the *Exercises*, even though M. Metz assures us that Saint Gertrude was certainly not acquainted with it (p. 284, note 37). We know from the *Herald* that at least one ceremony of consecration took place at Helfta on a feast of our Lady; see *Legatus*, Lib. V, cap. 5, p. 536.

9 *Legatus*, Lib. II.

10 Dom Pierre de Puniet, *Le Pontifical romain, histoire et commentaire* (Paris, 1931), II, p. 175.

11 See fourth Exercise, note 9.

12 Metz, *La consécration des vierges*, pp. 353-354.

13 Puniet, *Le Pontifical romain*, II, p. 175.

14 *La lumière de la Divinité, révélations de la Soeur Mechtilde de Magdebourg*, translated from the German by the Monks of Solesmes (Poitiers, 1878), Livre VII, chap. 30, p. 309. This chapter is one of several which are omitted in the English translation by Lucy Menzies.

15 *Liber Specialis Gratiae*, Pars II, cap. 38, pp. 186-187; see also Pars IV, cap. 31, pp. 289-290.

16 Metz, *La consécration des vierges*, p. 218, note 193.

COMMENTARY: FOURTH EXERCISE

1 *Liber Specialis Gratiae*, Pars IV, cap. 16, p. 273.

2 *Ibid.*, cap. 17, pp. 274-275.

3 *Ibid.*, Pars III, cap. 6, p. 205. See also Pars IV, cap. 60, p. 315; Pars V, cap. 20, p. 351.

4 Puniet, *Le Pontifical romain*, II, chap. IV, pp. 63 ff. *Pontificale Romanum* (Mechlin, 1934), De benedictione abbatis, pp. 202-209. *The Rule of St. Benedict*, Chap. 58, pp. 130-133.

5 See list of liturgical texts (third Exercise).

6 A similar rite occurs in the ceremony of the blessing of an abbot, where the seven penitential psalms precede the litany. See *Pontificale Romanum*, pp. 215 ff.

7 *The Rule of St. Benedict*, Chap. 58, pp. 131-133.

8 Metz, *La consécration des vierges*, p. 201.

9 *Pontificale Romanum*, De benedictione abbatis, p. 206.

10 *Legatus*, Lib. V, cap. 34, p. 610.

11 *Ibid.*, Lib. II, cap. 11, p. 62.

12 Paul Franche, *Sainte Hildegarde* (Paris, 1903), p. 21.

13 For an allusion to her profession, see *Legatus*, Lib. III, cap. 44, p. 210; that of Saint Mechtild is alluded to in *Liber Specialis Gratiae*, Pars V, cap. 30, p. 366.

COMMENTARY: FIFTH EXERCISE

1 *Legatus*, Lib. II, cap. 3, pp. 62 ff.

2 *Liber Specialis Gratiae*, Pars I, cap. 8, p. 26; cap. 20, p. 71; cap. 35, p. 116; etc. *The Revelations of Mechthild of Magdeburg*, Part I.3, p. 8; Part IV.19, p. 115; etc.

3 *Legatus*, Lib. I, cap. 5, p. 19; etc.; Lib. III, cap. 74, p. 257; Lib. IV, cap. 25, p. 382.

4 See commentary on the sixth Exercise, p. 108, note 2; and text, p. 132.

5 Saint Bernard, *Sermones in Cantica*, Sermo VIII, Migne, P.L., Vol. CLXXXIII (Paris, 1854), col. 810 ff. For an (abridged) English version, see: Saint Bernard, *On the Song of Songs*, translated by a Religious of C.S.M.V. (London, 1952), Sermon 8, pp. 30-32.

6 Emmanuel, *Les Exercices de Sainte Gertrude*, pp. 242-243, note 6-9.

7 *Legatus*, Lib. II, cap. 5, pp. 68-71; Lib. V, cap. 25, pp. 581-583.

8 Reginald Garrigou-Lagrange, O.P., *The Three Ages of the Interior Life*, II (St. Louis, 1951), pp. 353-355.

The Exercises of Saint Gertrude

COMMENTARY: SIXTH EXERCISE

1 Sister Florence Feeney, O.S.B., "Love's response: the *Exercises* of St. Gertrude," in *The Benedictine Review*, IX, No. 1 (January, 1954), quoted with the Editor's permission.

2 "Rara hora et parva mora." Saint Bernard, *Sermones in Cantica*, Sermo XXIII.15, col. 892. See *Legatus*, Lib. III, cap. 74, p. 257; *Exercitia*, p. 79.

3 First Exercise, p. 9; fourth Exercise, pp. 59-60.

COMMENTARY: SEVENTH EXERCISE

1 In one of the allegories by Mechtild of Magdeburg, the personification of love and the other virtues is particularly striking. See *The Revelations of Mechthild of Madgeburg*, Part VII, 48, pp. 245 ff.

2 *Legatus*, Lib. III, cap. 46, pp. 213 ff. Saint Mechtild gives us an example of the same device in *Liber Specialis Gratiae*, Pars III, cap. 29, pp. 233-234.

3 For a brief parallel passage, see *Legatus*, Lib. IV, cap. 17, p. 355.

4 *Ibid.*, Lib. II, cap. 1, pp. 59 ff.

Index of selected subjects
from the text of the Exercises

INDEX OF SELECTED SUBJECTS

A NOTE ON THE TYPE

IN WHICH THIS BOOK IS SET

This book is set in Times Roman, a Linotype face created by Stanley Morrison, world-famous typographical authority. Designed for the London *Times* which demanded a type face that should be clear and legible, precise but not mechanical, having a high letter but not condensed, of a "color" suitable for any paper or printing process, with character but not with annoying characteristics. Notice the clear, open characters of Times Roman. This is the secret of its clear printing on any paper, whether it be on the coarsest of newsprint or the finest coated paper. This book was composed and printed by the Wickersham Printing Company of Lancaster, Pa., and bound by Moore and Company of Baltimore. Typography and design by Howard N. King.